This book is donated in
loving memory of
Cobey England
"Live to dance so that
you may dance
to live"

FREDERICK
COUNTY
**PUBLIC
LIBRARIES**

Books Promiscuously Read

Books Promiscuously Read

◆

READING
AS A
WAY OF LIFE

Heather Cass White

FARRAR, STRAUS AND GIROUX   NEW YORK

Farrar, Straus and Giroux
120 Broadway, New York 10271

Owing to limitations of space, all acknowledgments for permission to reprint
previously published material can be found on page 162.

Library of Congress Cataloging-in-Publication Data
Names: White, Heather Cass, author.
Title: Books promiscuously read : reading as a way of life / Heather Cass White.
Description: First edition. | New York : Farrar, Straus and Giroux, 2021. |
    Includes bibliographical references.
Identifiers: LCCN 2021002655 | ISBN 9780374115265 (hardcover)
Subjects: LCSH: Literature—Appreciation. | Books and reading. |
    Literature and society.
Classification: LCC PN47 .W56 2021 | DDC 801/.3—dc23
LC record available at https://lccn.loc.gov/2021002655

Designed by Abby Kagan

For Robert Baker, *il miglior lettore*

A participatory corps is required.

—C. D. Wright, *Cooling Time*

Contents

A NOTE ON QUOTATION

Much of what readers think and say occurs in the words of others. In order to stay true to this experience of the reader's mind, I have left most of this book's quoted material unattributed in the main text. Complete references to all quotations will be found at the end.

I

◆

Propositions

1. Reading creates minds in its image.

A whole life, "right alongside the rest of [a] life," can be lived inside books. A life spent reading affirms the feeling it also creates, that books have "insides." A book is a "commodity inclusive / of the idea, the art object, the exact spot in which to live." We shelter there, or cower, or delight, or rage; we "dream with our eyes open," "separate and alone and yet intimately connected, mind-wired to distant things," "driving to the interior," from which we emerge "changed, healed, charged." Reading is individual, "the repository of [one's] inner self-relation," and it is communal: into that "single, immobile and solitary act," "all the powers of the cult of the gods have migrated." These powers are thrilling and dangerous, "a betrayal of the dominant order of things," and they are tender, our lives "held precariously in the seeing / hands of others." "It seems, in the last analysis, to have something to do with our self-preservation."

2. Readers should read.

Reading is one portal among many to rich inner experience. It is one mode among many of living the life that one has, astonishingly and against all odds, been given. Not everyone has to be a reader. If reading is what William James called a "living option" in one's life, however, if it is a possibility felt to be open to any extent, then it is good to do it with one's whole attention, while also asking nothing in particular of it, or of one's self, while doing it. Reading in this way is doing something, not failing to do something else. It can be surprisingly hard to hold on to this truth, however powerfully we experience it.

3. A reader should read every day.

People who like to read should do more of it. The reasons not to do it are endless, and people who think of themselves as book lovers, who have the wherewithal to choose how they use their time, are often the most in thrall to them. Reading is time-consuming and requires focus. One has to sit down to do it, in a quiet place. Too many people actually do lack the essential conditions for reading: time and silence. These are scarce resources. For the many other people who have these advantages, however, and for the smaller number who would call themselves readers, and who yet do not actually read in any sustained way, much of what looks like external pressure is actually the mask of an internal reluctance. Reading without purpose is playful, and play is not easy for adults. It induces a "perfectly useless concentration" that will not make the reader seem or feel productive. There are no prizes for reading, no pay raises for it, no competitive advantage in it. It accomplishes nothing.

All reading has to offer is a particular, irreplaceable internal experience. Readers should keep faith that that experience is enough. We should fight for it, especially if the fight is against our own sense of obligation to the world. Reading is an activity, a doing something, that takes place in D. W. Winnicott's "potential space," a region neither inside nor outside the self, but a paradoxical place that is both. It is an adult form of the dreamy, abstracted play of children that happens in "an area that cannot be easily left, nor can it easily admit intrusions." We go there because we have a self that must be articulated, and because we do not have a self until we find its articulation. We think and are thought, dream and are dreamed by what we read. "The actual world does shear away," says C. D. Wright. "The reader is there for the duration, and leaves with reluctance."

4. We read elsewhere.

Reading as I mean it here has one distinctive feature: in doing it the reader steps aside from the "actual world." That step can be characterized in a number of ways—as escape, transcendence, respite, rejection, subversion, suspension, or otherwise. All of these terms will describe a single reader's experience of reading over time, often simultaneously. What matters is the reader's recognition that she *is* stepping aside, and her commitment to following whatever path that step reveals. No one can tell another person with certainty what kind of book will allow her to wander in this way. Thoreau prescribes books "we have to stand on tiptoe to read." Jane Hirshfield says "only words that enlarge the realm of the possible merit borrowing our attention from the world of the actual and the living." Each reader finds a personal canon of such challenging and enlarging books and spends a lifetime, if he or she is lucky, revising it. No two canons will be the same, but in the shared experience of encountering language (at least some of the time) at the edges of our capacity to understand, and feeling (with whatever initial balance of guilt and excitement) that we have withdrawn for a while from the world's claims on us, we are reading.

5. "Why not be alone together?"

Imagine that in reading you take part in *communitas*: "a spontaneous gathering of persons who identify themselves and one another as members of a unified body . . . [that] evolves . . . out of the desire of its participants to get to the bottom of the very mystery that brings them together." In its collective sense this is the "participatory corps" required to keep reading alive as a form of experience. Imagine that somewhere a wheel turns and continues to turn only so long as people are reading. The complementary term to *communitas* is *civitas*, an institution "dependent on rulers to protect its integrity and authorities to guide its beliefs." We consent to live in a given *civitas*, however mixed our feelings may be about the terms and conditions our participation entails. We also participate in *communitas*, as expressed in a potentially infinite number of spontaneously formed and dissolved communities of interest and inquiry. The lines between our civil and communal lives are not clearly drawn, and the lines as we feel them in our own lives may look entirely different to others. While expressions of *communitas* are notoriously subject to co-optation by the rulers of *civitas* for their own ends, no *civitas*, however enlightened, can answer the questions that drive *communitas*. Reading is a way to keep asking vital questions in the company of others.

6. Reading will not save us.

By its nature *communitas*, including its expression as people who read, promises nothing, least of all a better self or world. Reading may have *benefits* (we hear often about a heightened sense of empathy, an alertness to logic and nuance, and a lengthened attention span) but is not a *virtue*. Goodness (a refusal to inflict suffering, a curiosity about the lives of others, an inclination to serve?) has never been associated with the literary mind more than any other. Violence is perpetrated by and in the name of readers. Reading conduces to inwardness, but many good people are not inward, and many inward people are not good.

7. Our reading is historical.

If we don't know that reading makes us or the world good, why do we care if no one does it? Why in particular should we be alarmed by reports of reading's demise as a widespread pastime? Perhaps we shouldn't, exactly. If reading disappears, something else will take its place. Not its precise place; if reading were lost, much that is valuable would be lost. But we would get over it, or successive generations would, and whatever replaced it would have advantages we can't imagine. Writing itself is a technology, and a fairly recent one, that decimated older forms of communication and experience, and created new ones that shape the world as we currently understand it. "*Homo sapiens*," writes Walter Ong, "has been in existence for between 30,000 and 50,000 years. The earliest script dates from only 6,000 years ago." "Of all the many thousands of languages," he continues,

—possibly tens of thousands—spoken in the course of human history only around 106 have ever been committed to writing to a degree sufficient to have produced literature, and most have never been written at all. . . . Even now hundreds of languages in active use are never written at all: no one has worked out an effective way to write them. The basic orality of language is permanent.

For those many preliterate millennia human culture had its own orally based thought-world, as it still does. While writing brings with it unique capacities for abstract thought and linear reasoning, it is difficult for a literate mind to imagine the costs it has entailed to orally based knowledge structures. It is impossible even to name such structures once the mind has been (as ours have all been) permeated with writing: "Thinking of oral tradition or a heritage of oral performance, genres and styles as 'oral literature' is rather like thinking of horses as automobiles without wheels."

8. The history of reading is flowing, and flown.

Debates about the power, pitfalls, and proper use of this new technology underlie Western philosophy and remain contentious today. Socrates, "speaking" in a dialogue that descends to us entirely by means of Plato's writing, warns of the inevitable cost to human consciousness when we fix knowledge outside our speaking selves:

If men learn [writing], it will implant forgetfulness in their souls; they will cease to exercise memory because they rely on

that which is written, calling things to remembrance no longer from within themselves, but by means of external marks.
What you have discovered is a recipe not for memory, but for
reminder.

Members of the generation that has lost knowledge of basic math-
ematics to omnipresent calculators, and of phone numbers to cell
phone storage, might object that Socrates is here right about the
fragility of memory, but too alarmed about the consequences of
that fragility. What is so bad about forgetting if things are in fact
written down?

Socrates's answer is that what is lost when the human interlocutor disappears is not the content of what he has to say, but
the context that makes what he has to say meaningful. The diminished capacity of writing to *teach*, in other words, is what is at
stake. He explains:

> Written words . . . seem to talk to you as though they were intel-
> ligent, but if you ask them anything about what they say, from
> a desire to be instructed, they go on telling you just the same
> thing forever. And once a thing is put in writing, the composi-
> tion, whatever it may be, drifts all over the place, getting into
> the hands not only of those who understand it, but equally of
> those who have no business with it; it doesn't know how to ad-
> dress the right people, and not address the wrong.

From this perspective, a book in the hands of people who
can read is a difficult force to control, a potential pathogen with
limitless undefended hosts to infect. Even worse, words themselves, separated from the breath that incarnated them, become
the objects of our contemplation. Marks on a page, designed

to be simple transmitters, incidental vessels for the sacred fire of speech, have themselves drawn our focus and proliferated into complex systems of their own that compete for our worshipful attention. If language "is both a map of the world and its own world," readers are obsessive cartographers, moving always on the border of two spheres. Nietzsche writes approvingly that "only just now . . . is it dawning on people that they have propagated a colossal error with their belief in language. Luckily, it is too late for the development of reason, which rests upon that belief, to be reversed."

9. Reading is a danger to reason.

There is surprisingly little disagreement about reading's capacity to drive us right out of our minds. So well understood is the connection between reading and madness that Cervantes only needs one sentence to establish a plausible basis for Don Quixote's many hundreds of pages' worth of misadventures:

> In short, our gentleman became so caught up in reading that he spent his nights reading from dusk till dawn and his days reading from sunrise to sunset, and so with too little sleep and too much reading his brains dried up, causing him to lose his mind.

Two and a half centuries, one continent, and an entire culture later, Emily Dickinson describes her family's parallel understanding, telling her friend Thomas Wentworth Higginson: "[My father] buys me many Books—but begs me not to read them—because he fears they joggle the Mind."

10. Books are a realm of unreason.

Even as we have agreed as a culture to let words, in Plato's phrase, "drift all over the place," we live with an anxiety around the act of unsupervised reading, as though books have a life and a will of their own. Our feelings about the disposal of unwanted books reflect that sense. Like flags, books require special handling. They may be burned, in spectacular, emblematic, purifying fires. They may be preserved in specially built, temperature-controlled buildings, tended by trained professionals who regulate access to them. They may simply accumulate because it is impossible to put them in the trash. They are industrially pulped in a process readers don't like to think about.

Books bring out the animistic in people. We mistrust books' passive appearance as mere objects because the life they contain is so palpable. When a priest comes to burn the books of chivalry that have driven Quixote mad the books put up no fight, "waiting with all the patience in the world for the fire that threatened [them]." By contrast, the housekeeper helping the priest takes sensible precautions, imploring him to sprinkle the room with holy water so that "no enchanter, of the many in these books, can put a spell on us as punishment for wanting to drive them off the face of the earth." The housekeeper's fear is funny, and the joke still works. In a 1997 episode of *Friends*, Quixote's housekeeper is present in spirit when Joey tries to neutralize a scary book by putting it in the freezer.

11. Books are childish things.

Readers like to have books around because they continue to murmur after they have been read; they are living extensions of our minds into a space not wholly ours. A book is an object and a subject, a dweller halfway between alive and not alive. Children create such objects for themselves as a matter of course, long before they read. Toys of all kinds, blankets, and parts of their own bodies function as "transitional objects," developmental psychology's term for the objects children use to comfort themselves, which they invest with imaginative life.

The essential thing about a child's choice of transitional object is that the child makes it freely. She may choose the thing her mother suggests (by putting it in her crib), or the thing that most children choose (a thumb, say), but the child alone decides which object will be meaningful and goes about making it so. Reading, in the sense that most matters, must also happen freely. Like most of what we do in our lives lived here, "down, down in the terrestrial," our reading is circumscribed by factors beyond our control (How many languages do any of us read with ease? Which books do our peers read? What do current market forces think we ought to be reading?). All the same, if we concede that in the purest sense "the choice is never wide and never free," it is essential that our reading stays wild. It is not coincidental that students are bored by books they are required to read, even when those books began as scandals and guilty pleasures. It matters that we are frequently bored by the books we require ourselves to read. It may be that the most important function of required reading is to stimulate our resistance to it in the form of reading that is haphazard, spontaneous, whimsical, contrarian.

12. "Admittedly [we] err."

In a word, our reading is best when it is *promiscuous*, "Done or applied with no regard for method, order, etc.; random, indiscrimi-
nate, unsystematic" (*Oxford English Dictionary*). Books themselves
"drift all over the place" and so should we in our encounters with
them. Erring is the path, losing our way is the way. Reading allows
us to be surprised, and for that joyful and frightening privilege we
pay with our willingness to be wayward and partial, undefended
and incomplete. Any guides to reading this way will "only [have]
at heart your getting lost," and so will not look like guides at all.
To read is to wander in a direction, to yield to a current. Allowing
the words of another to flow through the mind is a way of playing
make-believe, not simply that what the words say is true, but that
the mind behind them is true, that there are minds besides our
own, with which we can play at merging and harmonizing.

13. USE USE USE / YR BODY AND YR MIND

Reading imaginative literature, which includes any number of
books called nonfiction or history or philosophy, and which may
or may not include reams of what are called novels, stories, and
poems, means finding it first. "We shall have to resign ourselves
to this," says Roberto Calasso, "that literature offers no signs, has
never offered any signs, by which it can immediately be identified." Calasso suggests instead that readers find signs in their own
bodies, citing Housman's sequence of words that "sets the hairs
of the beard on end," and the "new shiver" Hugo felt while reading Baudelaire. Examples of such testimony are plentiful. Despite
reading's bad physical reputation ("much reading is a weariness

of the flesh," warns Ecclesiastes), readers rely intimately on their bodies in registering the psychic effects of reading. Emily Dickinson is emphatic on the subject:

> If I read a book [and] it makes my whole body so cold no fire ever can warm me I know *that* is poetry. If I feel physically as if the top of my head were taken off, I know *that* is poetry. These are the only way I know it. Is there any other way.

Marianne Moore, searching for an adequate definition of "the genuine" that may be found in poetry, compares it to "hands that can grasp, eyes that can dilate, hair that can rise if it must." Our bodies read along with our minds; we feel with both the "force and beauty" of art's process. This is true also during the more frequent times that our reading is not accompanied by noticeable physical response. Adam Phillips observes that "in states of absorption, the . . . object that disappears is the body. The good-enough environment of the body can be taken for granted; it is most reliably present by virtue of its absence."

Our bodies, at rest or brought singingly to life, are our instruments in reading, keeping time in the background, playing and being played upon by the text. "Even and especially in our day, in our amnesiac land," affirms C. D. Wright, "poets are the griots, the ones who see that the word does not break faith with the line of the body." The line linking language and body is as fine and strong as spider silk, registering the least tremors on either end. Lines of writing need a pulse and a pace, a shapeliness to draw us in, and the promise of a full consciousness guiding them, different from our own but alike in fullness. They are lifelines in both directions.

14. Reading is a grown-up pleasure.

Reading is a home for sexual promise and longing. It is an education in the pleasures of sameness and strangeness, of bringing another mind to life, of feeling one's own self overlaid by and intermixed with another's. Mastery and skill are evanescent goals in the world of reading. Held to too long they become reading's opposite, power pursued by other means. Reading lays us as bare as we can stand to be. We come to it undefended, with only our capacity for response to guide us, or we don't come to it at all. In this way it is a simple and strict practice, one with infinite variations and turns, but no shortcuts and few signposts.

It does, however, reward dawdling and experimentation. Subterfuge, faithlessness, and fickleness are all intimate parts of the reader's life: "There are those who, while reading a book, recall, compare, conjure up emotions from other, previous readings. . . . This is one of the most delicate forms of adultery." Books are endlessly patient; they "stop somewhere, waiting for you." There is no penalty for abandoning or outgrowing one's old attachments in the world of literature, and no stigma accompanies widely ranging taste and an expansive array of partners to satisfy it. We mature as readers by becoming more present in a primal arena where we can test the objects of our desire by bringing to them the full range of our selves: our weakness, our aggression, our hunger, our "perfect contempt."

15. Reading is an act of self-determination.

"Books promiscuously read" is Milton's phrase for the reading he argues people should do, without interference from licensing bodies, despite authorities' fears that readers will be led into vice by reading the wrong books:

> Since . . . the knowledge and survey of vice is in this world so necessary to the constituting of human virtue, and the scanning of error to the confirmation of truth, how can we more safely and with less danger scout into the regions of sin and falsity than by reading all manner of tractates and hearing all manner of vice? And this is the benefit which may be had of books promiscuously read.

The sexual connotation of "promiscuous" did not predominate for another 250 years, but it is latent in Milton's metaphors: "I cannot praise a fugitive and cloistered virtue. . . . That virtue . . . which is but a youngling in the contemplation of evil, and knows not the utmost that vice promises to her followers, and rejects it, is but a blank virtue, not a pure; her whiteness is but an excremental whiteness." Milton did not mean that actual women should read freely, let alone that they should go out and experience "the utmost that vice promises to her followers." In the mid-seventeenth century the virtue that free access to books threatened belonged to the relatively small number of people, found mostly among the male members of the aristocratic and professional classes, who could read them. Good arguments, however, have a way of exceeding the imaginations of those who make them. Free minds require and shape free bodies, and vice versa; any social system with an interest in keeping bodies unfree is well advised to guard literacy carefully. Janie, the journeying heroine of *Their Eyes Were Watching God*, needs three marriages and a brush with violent death to learn what her author suggests she might have known a lot sooner: "she didn't read books so she didn't know that she was the world and the heavens boiled down to a drop."

16. Reading is insidious.

With respect to reading we live in a world unrecognizable to a man of Milton's day, but global literacy is still an elusive goal, and women are still excluded from it at grossly disproportionate rates. This is not accidental. The list of forces that have made literacy available and necessary on a vast scale is long: in the West, revolutions in printing technology, the entry of women into the commercial sphere and the expansion of public education that supported it, and the accompanying centuries-long shift in higher education away from classical to demotic languages, just to name three such forces, all made an exponentially increased number of texts accessible to an ever more heterogeneous body of individuals. As the number and variety of readers increased, so did the intensity of the debates about who ought to read what or be taught to read at all.

As well they might. Reading is insidious. It happens where no one else can see. One can read *to* another person, but not *for* him—it is done by one individual, silently. Those who love to do it and those who wish to regulate it are reacting to the same principle: reading is radically private. Its privacy is a mystery, because it exists out in the open, within anyone who reads, anywhere she does it, and because it takes place in a part of ourselves where we are unfixed, becoming, not quite a self that knows what boundaries it needs to protect. In that soft place there are no guarantees; "we must never assume that we know exactly what is happening when anyone else reads a book." Reading is an irritant to anyone who wants to maintain power over another, because reading is a form of self-possession that enmeshes us with others as subjects. "The discovery that you are the unrepeatable center of your own vision is simultaneous with the discovery that I am the center of my own." There is no cordoning off of sexual or civic freedom from this process. The ability to read means the power to absorb all messages, "valentines and messages of state; or soberer news."

17. "A light to read by—perfect!"

> Zeus . . . would not entrust the
> Fierce inexhaustible fire to the hands of men, who
>   must perish,
> Creatures engendered of ash trees, who dwell on the
>   face of the earth.
> But Prometheus, Iapetus's brave son, thoroughly
>   fooled him,
> For he stole inexhaustible fire, whose blaze can be seen
>   from
> Far, in a hollow cane, which offended profoundly the
>   mind of
> Zeus, who thunders Aloft, and his fond heart grew
>   very angry
> Seeing the twinkle of fire from afar among men, who
>   are mortal.
>
> —Hesiod, *Theogony*

18. "And once a thing is put in writing, the composition, whatever it may be, drifts all over the place."

Here is one idea, put into writing, that shaped a country, and the ethos of a people:

> We hold these truths to be self-evident, that all men are created equal, that they are endowed by their Creator with certain unalienable Rights, that among these are Life, Liberty and the pursuit of Happiness.

The danger of putting such an idea in writing is that, exactly as Plato predicts, it will speak to people for whom it was never meant, addressing the "wrong" listeners. Without the safeguarding of speech, delivered by a particular person to a carefully selected audience, the words say what they say to anyone at all, ignoring the implicit limits their authors may have imagined. For example, the printed statement "all men are created equal" might convince anyone who reads it that persons, regardless of the color of their skin, are equally endowed with unalienable rights by virtue of descending from a common Creator. In 1829 David Walker, a free Black man, was so convinced. "See your Declaration Americans!!!" he begins, in a pamphlet distributed throughout the southern slave states:

> Compare your own language . . . , extracted from your Declaration of Independence, with your cruelties and murders inflicted by your cruel and unmerciful fathers and yourselves on our fathers and on us . . . !!!!!!

The evident danger of the Declaration's "drifting" into the minds of the wrong persons, and the danger of Walker's language drifting further, was so immediate, and the potential consequences so disastrous, that lawmakers interested in preserving the distinction between the right audiences and wrong got straight to the heart of the matter. The historian Elizabeth McHenry reports:

> Legislators in Georgia and Louisiana . . . banned the distribution of all antislavery literature and abruptly enacted laws to control and prevent black literacy.

These laws continued a tradition of prohibiting Black literacy older than the nation itself:

> South Carolina.—Act of 1740: "Whereas, the having slaves taught to write, or suffering them to be employed in writing, may be attended with *great inconveniences;* Be it enacted, that all and every person and persons whatever, who shall hereafter teach or cause any slave or slaves to be taught to write . . . shall, for every such offense, forfeit the sum of one hundred pounds, current money."

19. Reading's origins are transgressive.

If Western mythology, from Prometheus, to Eve, to Milton's Satan, teaches one lesson, it is that knowledge is acquired in defiance of authority. Our mythic minds imagine that knowledge is a crime, a transgression of boundaries (whether marked or not) that leaves its possessor transformed, and exiled. Mary Shelley's *Frankenstein*, her tale of *The Modern Prometheus*, presents an allegory of this belief, setting its antihero Creature on a path to self-knowledge, and self-destruction, by having him commit the intellectual theft of learning to read. While a family teaches a child (the "right" audience) to read, the Creature (very much "wrong") eavesdrops:

> I soon perceived, that although the stranger uttered articulate sounds, and appeared to have a language of her own, she was neither understood by, or herself understood, the cottagers. . . . Presently I found . . . that she was endeavoring to learn their language; and the idea instantly occurred to me, that I should make use of the same instructions to the same end. . . . While I improved in speech, I also learned the science of letters, as it was taught to the stranger; and this opened before me a wide field for wonder and delight.

In a different country, at the same time that Shelley was making her fiction, two enslaved future writers, Frederick Douglass and William Wells Brown, were living under a not-at-all allegorical prohibition on reading and its attendant self-knowledge. Nearly thirty years after the publication of *Frankenstein*, their accounts of learning to read show them finding their solution, as Shelley's Creature does, in subterfuge. In coming to reading they live out the stuff of myth, stealing their learning, and with it, their freedom. Like Shelley's Creature, they find their culture's weak spot in its children. Douglass, in his 1845 *Narrative of the Life of Frederick Douglass*, writes:

> Mistress, in teaching me the alphabet, had given me the *inch*, and no precaution could prevent me from taking the *ell*.
> The plan which I adopted, and the one by which I was most

successful, was that of making friends of all the little white boys whom I met in the street. As many of these as I could, I converted into teachers.

Two years later *The Life and Escape of William Wells Brown* reports that its author,

> after considerable thinking upon the subject, . . . laid out 6*d*. for a spelling-book, and the other 6*d*. for sugar candy or barley sugar. Well, now, you will say that the one 6*d*. for the spelling-book was well laid out; and I am of the opinion that the other was well laid out too; for the family in which I worked for my bread had two little boys, who attended the school every day, and I wanted to convert them into teachers; so I thought nothing would act like a charm so much as a little barley sugar.

20. All transgressions are punished.

In myth and in life, self-knowledge, including its modern manifestation as the act of reading, carries a price. Prometheus, who gave us the means to read like Quixote, "from dusk till dawn," suffers a god's wrath:

> [Zeus] bound devious, wily Prometheus tightly in
> chains too
> Tough to escape from, terrible bonds, and he skewered
> his middle.
> Furthermore, on him he set a long-pinioned eagle to
> eat his
> Immortal liver.

Shelley's Creature, for having presumed to believe his literacy might bring him within the human family, finds instead that it shows him how far outcast he is. Worst of all, he finds that the knowledge reading brings him is irreversible:

> Sorrow only increased with knowledge. Oh, that I had forever remained in my native wood, nor known or felt beyond the sensations of hunger, thirst, and heat!
>
> Of what strange nature is knowledge! It clings to the mind, when it has once seized on it, like a lichen on the rock.

Frederick Douglass, neither myth nor fiction, nevertheless endures the punishments of both:

> As I read and contemplated . . . behold! that very discontentment which Master Hugh had predicted would follow my learning to read had already come, to torment and sting my soul to unutterable anguish. As I writhed under it, I would at times feel that learning to read had been a curse rather than a blessing. It had given me a view of my wretched condition, without the remedy. It opened my eyes to the horrible pit, but to no ladder upon which to get out. In moments of agony, I envied my fellow-slaves for their stupidity.

21. "The first demand any work of any art makes upon us is surrender."

To say that reading is private and solitary is only part of the truth. It is a shared privacy that consists in opening oneself to the presence of another person's use of language. It is a way of listening without having something to say, and as such it is a pathway to a widened interior space, filled with voices that resonate, that could not have originated in single speaker. Lewis calls the emptying, or quieting, of the self that must occur in order to engage in aesthetic experience (he is talking about painting) a "surrender" to the object of our attention: "We sit down before the picture in order to have something done to us, not that we may do things with it." The word "surrender" is just right. Reading is a voluntary loss of control, a chosen relinquishment of power.

In the sense that surrender means releasing something burdensome in order to be filled with something pleasurable, it looks like an easy choice. Rereading Barbara Pym rather than doing one's taxes is no hardship. The martial overtones of "surrender," however, are necessary to Lewis's description of what art requires of us, and suggest why, even for committed readers, ones who have not had to fight for the privilege of doing it freely, continuing to read may involve conflict. Surrender is not selective. Give yourself up, "get yourself out of the way," and what you rely on in yourself, the parts of yourself you have built up to keep you safe, go too. At the very least you have ceded time that will not come back. At worst you have, like Eve eating the apple, incorporated something that will change you in ways you don't expect or control. Reading doesn't happen to us, it happens with us, at our initiation and only of our continued volition. The pleasure of it is that it releases the creator in us: "One must be an inventor to read well." The pleasure, and the menace, is that we also invite in something wholly not us, that may not let us go, "tenacious, acquisitive, tireless, [that] cannot be shaken away." Reading requires an internal surrender, without promise of return in any external sense, and it requires navigating the world's demands, which will be different for every individual, but from which no individual is exempt, that we surrender our readerly freedom and put it to use. We must surrender while refusing to surrender our right to that surrender.

22. Reading is a morning's work.

"What should be man's *morning work* in this world?" asks Thoreau. He is looking at three rocks on his desk, "terrified" at the dusting they will henceforth need, having been brought inside. He has been brooding on overstuffed houses, darkly concluding that "a good housewife would sweep out the greater part of [our furniture] into the dust hole, and not leave her morning's work undone." But what is a *morning*, and what is *work*? *Walden* trains us by example to ask such questions. Thoreau's nominal project was to live a part of his life in seclusion, but he is never less secluded than when he is alone with his thoughts. When he goes to the woods his language goes with him, and *Walden* is the record of the exponential enrichment his words undergo in those conditions, freed from the constraints of social life. Thoreau says his own morning work in winter was to "take an axe and pail and go in search of water." He did not need to do this, in the sense that he would otherwise have had no water. His material privations were entirely chosen. He may nonetheless have needed to do it, in the sense that it taught him something he could learn in no other way. Part of what it taught him was the proliferating significance of the sentences with which he constructed a record of his time. For Thoreau, the axe and the pail are props, tangible elements of what is, at heart, a thought experiment: What will happen to a man and his language if they are left alone together?

The answer is that his words "grow double," grow treble, mean all that they say and much more that they don't. Axe and pail: cut and gather. Free what flows from what stays still. Fight through a cold that burns the tongue to a coolness that sustains the body. Is an axe a crude tool? Are its marks biting, sharp, and unbeautiful? Use it with whatever skill you have, because any tool will suffice if you have a goal. Cut ice in the morning, when your body is thirsty after sleep, when it is strongest after rest, when the mind is clearest of demands imposed on it from without, most focused on essentials. Morning work is an expenditure of the self at the moment it is most concentrated and purified by night's psychic labor. Use it wisely. Keep asking what morning work is. The answer can't be found with a single stroke of the axe or weighed against anything carried in a pail.

Unsurprisingly, Thoreau spent much of his time on Walden Pond reading. He even allows that reading, carefully delimited, is fit work for the morning:

> The student may read Homer or Aeschylus in the Greek without danger of dissipation or luxuriousness, for it implies that he in some measure emulate their heroes, and consecrate morning hours to their pages.

Of all his impractical proposals, Thoreau's suggestion that we "consecrate morning hours" to our reading is simultaneously one of his easiest, and the one most likely to encounter resistance among readers themselves. Few people tend to be more alert to the charges of "dissipation and luxuriousness" with respect to reading than the people who love it. We may not, like Thoreau, guard against it by restricting our "morning" reading to books written in classical languages, but we routinely restrict our reading in other ways. For example, no reading at all in the morning;

no reading until our "real" work is done; no reading that will not in some way "improve" us. In 1879 Nietzsche noted with displeasure:

> We have the conscience of a *hard-working* age: this does not allow us to give our best hours and mornings to art, even if it were the greatest and worthiest art. We consider it something for leisure, for recuperation: we devote to it the *left-over portion* of our time and our energies.

In 1996 a passionate reader proved him still correct:

> [Reading] was what I used to do through long evenings. Never mornings—even to one so self-indulgent, it seems slightly sinful to wake up and immediately sit down with a book—and afternoons only now and then. In daylight I would pay what I owed to the world. Reading was the reward, a solitary, obscure, nocturnal reward.

We should move a step beyond our preoccupation with dissipation and luxury where reading is concerned. The price is too high—it makes us read less. Even the pleasant aura of nocturnal dalliance we get for carving our life into daytime duty and nighttime reading, however attractively naughty it makes reading seem, is a distraction from the challenge of bringing our reading into the daylight. In the daylight we can affirm it, even and perhaps especially if only to ourselves, as a mode of living. We also serve who sit and read. It may help to keep in mind Thoreau's decision to devote his morning work to "axe and pail," so long as we acknowledge that "the pleasantry of a cat at pranks is in the language ten thousand times over." By means of one such prank, Kafka, just over fifty years after Thoreau's sojourn, articulates what readers, including Thoreau, know instinctively: "A book must be the axe for the frozen sea within us." The morning is now. The work is before us.

II

Play

Imagine a book is a toy. Toys come without rules, without instructions. Think of a ball: "It offers many interesting behaviors, which you may explore." A toy is the object of our playful attention, a means by which we can bring what is inside us into contact with what is outside. Toys are by nature mute. They don't tell us what they are for. They are for nothing until we put them to imaginative use. There are no wrong ways to use a toy, only ways that more or less closely match our imaginative needs of them. The greater those needs are, the richer our emotional ties to our toys will be, but we don't have responsibilities to toys that outlast our needs. The loss, theft, or destruction (especially our own destruction) of a toy may involve grief and regret, but a toy per se can't be wronged. Our responsibility to our toys ends when we say it does; "it / is permissible . . . to abandon / . . . the / roly-poly, when it shows signs of no longer being a pleas- / ure." An abandoned toy will wait forever, but any player can end its waiting. Our toys have no attachments to us that outlast our capacity to play with them. (Though we fantasize that things are otherwise. The *Toy Story* franchise is built on the perennial hope that our toys are more faithful to us than we are to them.) In use, a toy is an imaginative tool, and has potential meaning in every detail of its being.

If a book is a toy, reading is the game we play with it: "The game is not intrinsic in the toy; it is a set of player-defined objectives *overlaid* on the toy." A game requires the free assent of its players to a set of shared rules about the use of a toy. Those rules can be renegotiated, but the game proceeds only as long as the players agree to them. For example: A ball must be touched only with the hands, or never with the hands, and contact with the ball matters only within a marked field. Or: I am the daddy, you are the mommy, other players will be what the two of us decide they are, and the game is in effect only so long as no adult is within earshot. Or again: *x* number of my words have been typeset and disseminated by a particular sub-set of publishers, so now I am a professor and decide who else gets to be one.

Games by their nature look meaningless to non-players. Games *are* meaningless to non-players. The ludic becomes the ludicrous when seen from the outside, and only those who have agreed to the game's terms are inside it. (This is true even when the action of the game is to be the spectator of a game being played.) What are the rules of reading, and when and among what company do we agree to them? One of the most important of them is a refusal, or perhaps just an inability, to recognize the boundaries, intuitively obvious to most other people, that mark off the field of reading's play: for readers there are few meaningful distinctions of scale, intensity, or consequence between the everyday world and the world of books. For a certain kind of athlete, the white lines bounding the tennis court "make one little room, an every where." For the reader, the margins of the page enclose a universe coextensive, for a time, with any other she knows. Finding other players in the game of reading is one of its lifelong pleasures. The search for them has the advantage over most other games of being independent of time and place. In the shared play of reading the dead are as welcome as the living, the far as present as the near.

Everyone who has felt reading as a mode of life rather than a diversion from it is a player. Any trace they leave behind them of that feeling is an element of the game.

Some players are more skillful than others. It is not incidental that *Don Quixote*, the book that "contains within itself all the novels that have followed in its sublime wake," is about a reader. It is in fact about *the* reader, in the sense that Quixote is both a consummate reader, committed beyond parallel to inhabiting his readerly life, and an archetype of the readerly mind at play. Novels as we know them today exist to feed the same hunger that gnawed at Quixote, the gaunt knight who grows ever thinner as he rides out to remake the world in his books' image. The purity of his hunger—for stories, for imaginative immersion, for a world commensurate with the one he finds in his books—is the crux of Quixote's charisma, the reason no one has ever been able to stop talking about him, within his book or out of it. "As for your grace's valor, courtesy, deeds, and undertakings," notes Sancho, "there are different opinions. Some say, 'Crazy, but amusing'; others, 'Brave, but unfortunate'; and others, 'Courteous, but insolent'; and they go on and on so much in this vein that they don't leave an untouched bone in your grace's body or mine." Quixote is the best player who ever lived of a game whose rules only he, so far, has been able fully to follow, but that any reader will recognize.

His first move in the game is the one readers make instinctively, and the one that establishes his field of play as marked off from the world non-players live in: he assigns to his books the time and attention properly assigned to "work." To put it another way, he not only "spent his nights reading from dusk till dawn" (a forgivable folly), but he "spent . . . his days reading from sunrise to sunset" (a serious violation of rules of adult citizenship). In essence, he inverts the playing field of reading. The people around him understand the kind of reading he does, his wide-eyed dives into chivalric romances, to be a game played, if at all, in time demarcated as "leisure." The prize for this game, insofar as they can imagine it has one, is a brief respite from the rigors of playing the real game, of living itself, in which the worthwhile prizes of property, power, and reputation are to be won. For Quixote, the world outside of his books is an illusory world, an elaborate trial put in the way of the serious contender, designed to be seen through only by the best players. The rules of Quixote's game are inflexibly at odds with the rules of everyone else's. The more skillfully he plays, the more "chimerical, foolish, senseless, and turned inside out" he will look.

James Carse, in *Finite and Infinite Games*, proposes a fruitful distinction:

> There are at least two kinds of games. One could be called finite, the other infinite.
>
> A finite game is played for the purpose of winning, an infinite game for the purpose of continuing play.

Quixote is a genius at continuing play. There are no circumstances he cannot absorb into his game. Everything he encounters can be folded seamlessly into the world of his books; the more outrageously that power to enfold is tested, the more durable the game becomes. His exchange with Sancho about "the helmet of Mambrino" is emblematic of his dexterity and his willfulness, his madness and his power:

"Tell me, do you not see that knight coming toward us, mounted on a dappled gray and wearing on his head a helmet of gold?"

"What I see and can make out," responded Sancho, "is just a man riding a donkey that's gray like mine, and wearing something shiny on his head."

"Well, that is the helmet of Mambrino," said Don Quixote.

Quixote's enemies are not the powerful enchanters, malevolent giants, and base insulters of his honor he believes surround him. On the contrary—those figures are the necessary fellow players in his game, and his invention of them is the means by which he continues to play. His invention of them is the game itself. Rather, his true enemies are innkeepers, whose principal function in the novel is to bring his play to an end. The poet Eleanor Chai, quoting Winnicott, says that "the opposite of play in a child isn't work. // The opposing force to play in a child is reality." The opposing force to play in *Don Quixote* is also reality:

> "Pay me what you owe me," [said the innkeeper,] "and leave off your stories and chivalries; I don't care about anything but earning my living."
>
> "You are a fool and a bad innkeeper," responded Don Quixote.

Quixote is wrong in one respect. The innkeeper is playing his part as an innkeeper well, not badly. Whether that is a foolish part to play depends on the game in which one is engaged. For Quixote, beatings, starvation, penury, and humiliations are the conditions of play, not signs of defeat. For Quixote there is no defeat except a lapse in faithfulness to his books. The world calls him mad, and he claims that madness as divinest sense. Every bruise he endures in its service endears him further to subsequent generations of readers, confirms newly that he is a "parody . . . become a paragon."

But within his own story, to whom is he a paragon? What are the costs of his peerless ability to prolong play, to insist that the game he plays never end, and that everyone and everything he encounters is part of it? Quixote's adventures embody the darker aspects of Carse's "vision of life as play and possibility":

> To be playful is not to be trivial or frivolous, or to act as though nothing of consequence will happen. . . . It is, in fact, seriousness that closes itself to consequence, for seriousness is a dread of the unpredictable outcome of open possibility. To be serious is to press for a specified conclusion. To be playful is to allow for possibility whatever the cost to oneself.

The physical toll of Quixote's and Sancho Panza's quests is gruesome. They starve, they freeze, they are attacked in battles and in pranks, and they are more than once left bloody, broken-boned, and nearly toothless. Their calamities are played mostly for laughs, but harder to laugh off are the injuries suffered by the many characters in the novel whose only mistake is to appear alongside Quixote. For every admiring listener caught up in Quixote's passion for honor above all things, made indulgent by what he or she sees as his comic unfitness for the world, there are several more who exclaim, with good reason, that "it was an evil moment and a cursed hour when this knight errant came into my house." Early in their travels, Quixote and Sancho encounter an apprentice being beaten unmercifully by his master. Quixote intercedes on behalf of the apprentice, having the master swear a patently worthless oath to treat the apprentice better thereafter. Quixote, satisfied, rides away, leaving the apprentice to suffer a beating all the more vicious for the interruption. Later, knight and squire encounter a group of novitiates carrying a Madonna along a country road; driven into a frenzy by his belief that the statue is a captive maiden, Quixote attacks them. Shepherds lose flocks to Quixote's violence. Even innkeepers earn the reader's sympathy, robbed as they invariably are of the costs of their hospitality by Quixote's blithe insistence that rendering service to a knight like himself is reward enough for any honorable person.

If Quixote is admirable it is not because he has a beneficent effect on those around him. He is heedless of his own life, in ways that also damage other people. His madness unfits him for any world except the one he invents, but he lives in the one he shares with others. The most trenchant modern commentary on the ethical incoherence of Quixote's questing existence is George Saunders's twelve-page story "My Chivalric Fiasco." In it, a man named Ted works at a medieval-themed restaurant, dressing up as a knight and enacting nightly jousts for the diners' entertainment. Ted, a hapless man burdened with the care of an ailing family, gets into character (as is corporate policy) by taking a drug called KnightLyfe®, which, much like Quixote's reading, dries up his brains and compels him to proclaim Truths. One night, he witnesses his boss raping a coworker. She begs him to keep it secret, and his boss offers them hush money they both badly need. Ted, by nature more of a Sancho Panza than a Don Quixote, is inclined to take the money. Nevertheless, two nights later, under the influence of KnightLyfe®, he proclaims to the crowd a Truth: "That Don Murray had taken Foul Advantage of Martha, placing, against her Will, his Rod into her Womanhood on TorchLightNight." Quixotic nobility goes as well for Ted as it usually does for Quixote. Having told the truth, Ted is beaten, fired, and left to face his newly impoverished family. As the drug wears off, he reflects:

> I attempted to Comfort myself, saying I had done Right, and served Truth, and shewn good Courage. But 'twas no Comfort in it. It was so weird. Why had I even done That? I felt like a total dickBrain.

Hero or dickBrain—a straightforward accounting of the net effects of his actions in the world leaves us no closer to deciding Quixote's true nature than the characters in the novel get through their endless discussion. Sancho throws up his hands, and so should we. It is a false opposition, and beside the point. Quixote's questing is the manifestation of an inner game, ardently played, that calls on all of him, aggression and cruelty included. There is no prize in the game except its continuance, no advancement or gain beyond "the passage of the mind from one thought to the next, and its ever deeper immersion into the same thought." Whether or not this is admirable, it is the heart of reading.

◆

To be toyed with is painful, and to get played for a fool, as Sancho Panza knows better than most, is humiliating. But to be played with is a joy, and to be played upon by the right person or thing, as Quixote's endless appetite for such play vividly shows, is exhilarating. Books make instruments of us; we are the means of their music. Sentences are scores, patterns to evoke tune. The music we make out of them depends on our tradition, temperament, and training, and most of all our particular instrument, each reader left with, in the end, her unique "home-made flute / [with] the weirdest scale on earth." Or maybe sentences are rain, playing on the infinitely varied surfaces it hits as it falls, percussive, flowing, loud, quiet. So, we are the surfaces, with channels and flats and minutely textured waterways revealed in their subtlety by what flows over and between and through us. The voice that becomes ours as we read is the meeting of sentence and inner instrument, the striking of object on object with collision's infinite possibility for sound, and it is the silences that open when objects miss one another and slide past. Everything we think and feel and know and expect and fear and dismiss and long for retunes our instrument moment by moment. This might be a description of consciousness itself. One pleasure of reading is that it is an arena small and distinct enough that we can focus our attention on, and so stay aware of, the intimate responsiveness of what is inside us to what is outside. It is an arena in which we can play and be played.

The writing we come back to, that plays us most richly, is characterized by intention. Intention is not quite a synonym for control. Intention can encompass chance and error and exists in shifting relation to skill. Say rather that intention is the palpable trace of a living mind, urged by a personal necessity out of which it selects its tools. It is not necessary to love or agree with or even much approve of a writer's intentions to nevertheless feel them at work and enjoy the play of the pattern they make as they sift through the reading mind. There are so many patterns to enjoy. There are so many selves with which to enjoy patterns. There is no need to establish a standard or identify a template: writing that makes music in us need not make it in anyone else or make it in the anyone else that we are at any other time. Because our reading is kaleidoscopic, any one sentence can give rise to multiple patterns. The mind plays with language, the interchange of eye and mind proceeding more strangely and less straightforwardly than it seems. Our inevitable misrememberings of what we read signal not our faultiness, but the dynamic process that reading is.

Moreover, the reader is not the only one at play in reading. If sentences cohere in a Newtonian universe of stable coordinates, they nevertheless originate in, and draw the reader back into, the quantum foam of phonetic play. The mind is active on both scales, large and small, at once. In reading we absorb and parse ideas, themes, story line, and structure, large-scale patterns that unite the many reading sessions it takes us to experience the whole of a book like *Don Quixote*. Simultaneously, however, we read on the moment-to-moment micro-scale of word, letter, and sound, particles winking in and out of existence according to the quality of our attention to them. Part of reading is accretive, language building up in the mind to form the book we draw from the pages before us and subsequently carry within us. But another part of reading (the basis of the accretive part) lives only in the present, is a transient experience that exists only in the now and now and now as we do it. Love of that impossible-to-hold experience is why readers also tend to be habitual rereaders. We read in part to find out what happens, but even more so to be part, over and over again, and never twice in exactly the same way, of its happening.

It is customary to think about qualities like alliteration, assonance, meter, and rhyme in the context of poetry, a genre in which we expect that the sound of language will be as consequential for our delight and understanding as its denotation. Modern lyric poetry, proceeding usually in short, concentrated bursts of densely worked sound, provides an inviting playing field for the close reader who wants to pay attention to as many facets of language at once as she can. Jorie Graham describes the interwoven physical and intellectual joy a single word, slowly considered, can bestow:

> and I thought about that word *expense*→and sympathy like a baby animal leaning into the sound of words because I had vocal cords→and they asked for that→and something was down there in me I myself barely owned→but which truly thrilled if a word was uttered→and I got it right

That thing "down there" in us that we "barely own," that capacity to imitate and respond to and play with language, to take it apart and put it back together many different ways, simultaneously, before we even know we have done it, is what poetic language stirs. Our sudden awareness of that capacity is what we feel when we call writing "poetic." If we agree that poetry "is that which is lost . . . in translation," it is because that feeling of getting it "right," which is to say receiving and re-creating the language complexly, at levels we can and cannot easily name, is diminished when a work is translated out of its original language. A line from Elizabeth Bishop's "At the Fishhouses," "it makes one's nose run and one's eyes water," is not quite the same line in a language in which "one's" and "nose" are not anagrams of each other. The title itself is not the same title without the eye-distracting pair of *h*'s in the middle of its principal word. In the realm of poetry, every facet of language's sound in the mind and appearance on the page is part of our aesthetic experience. At least, in reading poetry we are open to the *possibility* that each facet is an essential part of the work's nature, and cannot be altered without affecting every other facet. A Monet in which the brush left different corrugations in the paint would not be the Monet as we know it; a poem (as we tend currently to understand poems) put into words other than the poet's may be a work of art with virtues of its own, but it is not interchangeable with the original poem.

In practice, all written language, whether designated "poetry" or not, plays with and on and among aural and visual qualities. The feeling we get of a writer's awareness of those qualities, the extent to which we sense him marshaling them into pattern according to plan, is integral to what we mean by a writer's skill. Our sense of companionship in reading, of having found a mind to play with, often occurs irrespective of what a writer has to say. It is in her attention to its saying that we meet her. In prose, when that attention is palpable at every end of reading's scale, from the widest narrative and thematic sweep to the smallest cluster of its phonemes, its effects can be dazzling. And better than dazzling—there are moments when reader and writer can become united in feeling language, playing like "a cat at pranks," take writing in directions just outside of conscious intention. Such moments are difficult to describe, and difficult to prove satisfactorily. They are by nature personal to the individual reader, and occur in the twilight area where chance and intention become indistinguishable in a work of art. A cat at pranks is not interested in being caught. Caught, it is no longer at pranks at all. Isolating and explaining an instance of language at play stops the very motion that first drew one in, as "expanded explanation tends to spoil the lion's leap."

Nevertheless, an example may help. Don DeLillo's *Underworld*, an eight-hundred-plus-page landmark (and doorstop) of contemporary fiction, is an unusually rich medium in which to watch language, at its macro level, build a portrait of a country and its citizens, and, at the same time, at its micro level, seduce the ear away from the sense of that structure toward a pure pleasure in the music of its letters. On one hand, *Underworld* is a story about people (J. Edgar Hoover, Lenny Bruce, a narrator named Nick, an artist named Klara); places (the Bronx, the Southwest, toxic waste dumps, highways, hotels, and suburban houses); and things (language, trash, violence, technology, history, art, aging). It asks the reader to weave together fictitious people and events with fictionalized versions of real ones, to create an intricate portrait of postwar American anxiety and drive. On the other hand, *Underworld* is a bravura performance by a writer for whom the sound of language is its own event, with an independent logic that guides the story and, with it, both reader and writer. Any given passage of *Underworld*'s prose is a gift to the reader's ear, alive with a music of its own. A representative clause, "many chesty bureaucrats with interchangeable heads" hums the tune of the short *e* audible in "many," "chesty," and "heads," showing itself impishly even where it doesn't sound, in the *ea* of "bureaucrats" and "changeable." Sound-play is the atomic fuel of DeLillo's writing, present everywhere: "that whistles up out of unsuspected whim"; "how much summer and dust the mind can manage to order up from a single Latin letter lying flat"; "the voice is . . . mainly wham and whomp."

One phrase in particular brings together some of the novel's most powerful themes by means of an especially resonant piece of sound-play. In the scene it punctuates, J. Edgar Hoover has just emerged from a bath:

> Edgar turned . . . and saw himself unexpectedly in a full-length
> mirror, across the room, in his white robe and soft slippers, and
> he was startled by the image.

Of course it was him, but him in the guise of a macro-cephalic baby, sexless and so justborn as to be, in essence, unearthly.

Mother Hoover's cuddled runt.

The phrase "Mother Hoover's cuddled runt" has many tricks up its sleeve. In the context of the story, it telegraphs, in four short words, Edgar's self-loathing: the knowledge, which he holds just at bay, of the helplessness that feeds his need to control others by keeping meticulous track of their secrets. By extension, it gestures toward the anti-sex, misogynist nature of the surveillance culture he commands. In his ever more technologically sophisticated regime of weaponized information systems, Edgar, and the state he stands for, vilifies exactly those boundaryless, unrecordable, bodily intimacies on which the mother-child relationship is built. That vilification is a cornerstone of the modern America *Underworld* envisions, in which the future belongs to arenas "completely free of human presence," in which "the system flows forever onward, automated to a priestly nuance," and bodies—particularly female ones—are turned into waste. "Mother Hoover's cuddled runt" is able to do so much work in so few words because of the catchiness of the words themselves. It borrows the rhythm of Mother Goose (Jáck and Jíll went úp the híll) to lend bounce and memorability to the ugly alliteration of "cuddled runt." Swift and punchy, "Mother Hoover's cuddled runt" lingers in the ear, summing up what went before, coloring what happens afterward.

Just discernible in that lingering is "cuddled runt"'s strongest and slipperiest stroke. Hiding within it, and impossible to forget once heard, is a different, more sinister phrase: "ruddled cunt." Where does that shadow phrase sound? In something like Nietzsche's "third ear," the organ that tells the reader "there is *art* in every good sentence—art that wants to be figured out insofar as the sentence wants to be understood!" What does the easy consonantal back and forth of "cuddled runt / ruddled cunt" want us to understand? That for Edgar and the particular masculine world he represents, our physical origin in our mothers' bodies is an obscenity, to be feared and fled. That running alongside modernity's dream of unfettered, automated, smooth-running "priestly" systems is a world of bodies that attract and repulse and suffer and stain. That *Underworld*'s prose is playing a very deep game indeed, in which the reader is asked to follow what is not on the page as well as what is.

Did DeLillo *mean* this bit of evanescent sound-play? How can we know? And if he did not mean it, is it still there, generating meaning on its own? Is it real? Meeting DeLillo on this uncharted piece of aural territory epitomizes the reader's characteristic experience, of meeting another mind on the independent, unpredictable playing field of language itself. It highlights as well the crudity of our instinctive model of reading: player A (the author) has something to communicate to player B (the reader). If player A is a good passer, and B a good receiver, the thing communicated, inert like a football, will be smoothly transferred. But this is not how reading works. (DeLillo may not even think this is how *football* works. In *End Zone*, his novel on the subject, no one laughs when a player muses, "I sensed knowledge in the football. I sensed a strange power and restfulness. The football possessed awareness. The football knew what was happening.") In between writer and reader are words themselves, and underlying those words is a restless, seismic substratum of aural and emotional associations with unpredictable effects. The latent intrusion of "ruddled cunt" into Edgar's carefully guarded self-assessment, and into the reader's ear, still echoes at the book's end, when both the words *ruddle* and *cunt* actually appear, in close proximity to each other. In a climactic scene, one that brings together the whole preceding novel's meditations on misogyny, violence, poverty, and the commercial culture we have designed to efface the suffering they entail without actually curing it, a crowd gathers under a billboard in a Bronx neighborhood. They are there to witness a rumored miracle: the apparition of a girl who was raped and murdered nearby. The reader has been present at that rape, which is told from the rapist's point of view. His word for his victim is succinct: he calls her "cunt." Two pages later, on the billboard on which his victim's face is said to appear in a certain light, is an advertisement for orange juice. The juice "commands the eye, thick and pulpy with a ruddled flush that matches the madder moon."

Ruddled is an uncommon word, belonging, the OED says, to a group of words that "occur fewer than 0.01 times per million words in typical modern English usage." DeLillo, for whom "it remains the author's permanent duty to unbox the lexicon for all eyes to see," uses such words all the time. Or maybe they use him, "the words . . . commissioned, as it were, by language itself," the "beauty fl[ying] from the words themselves, the letters, consonants swallowing vowels, aggression and tenderness, a semi-self-re-creation from line to line, word to word, letter to letter." As it happens, the "semi-self-re-creation" of "cuddled runt" / "ruddled cunt" is the playful trace of DeLillo's own reading, an aggressive and tender tribute to his admirer David Foster Wallace. DeLillo's archives, like Wallace's, are housed at the Harry Ransom Center at the University of Texas. Early drafts of *Underworld*, collected in a folder marked *1991–1996*, show DeLillo working and reworking the scene of Edgar looking in the mirror. None of the ten or so drafts of the scene use the phrase "cuddled runt." Only a late, continuously typed, substantially finished (but undated) "second draft" contains the phrase. Where did DeLillo find it?

Nestled within another, even more gargantuan book. In September 1995, Little, Brown sent DeLillo a bound manuscript copy of Wallace's *Infinite Jest*. On page 114 of the published version, one finds this description of Hal Incandenza's "little buddy" Todd Ingersoll:

> this smart soft caustic kid, with a big soft eyebrowless face and unwrinkled thumb-joints, with the runty, cuddled look of a Mama's boy from way back

Did Wallace also hear the *r* and the *c* flip in describing that "runty, cuddled" kid? Maybe. The word *cunt* is not of much interest to *Infinite Jest*, popping up only as a verbal tic of a minor character. The word *ruddled*, by contrast, occurs, as it later will in *Underworld*, at the heart of the novel's climactic scenes. In the course of its final two hundred (non-footnote) pages, *Infinite Jest* uses *ruddled* four times, all in describing its hero Gately's final drug binge. The first three times it describes a quality of light, a bloody sunset outside coloring the hellish room in which Gately is trapped, and the blood-colored flames that eventually start flickering within. The fourth time, it describes the thing itself, Gately's own blood as it mixes with the drug that will deliver him into his last high: "He watched his own blood ruddle the serum as the pharmacist extended his thumb to ease the plunger back." Wallace read and annotated a bound manuscript copy of *Underworld*. His underlinings and notes show that he was keenly attuned to the sound of DeLillo's prose, but there is no note on "Mother Hoover's cuddled runt" to suggest he recognized the allusion to his own work. Perhaps DeLillo himself didn't recognize it. Nevertheless, *Underworld* itself registers what his ear learned while at play in Wallace's book, and invites the reader into the game.

◆

Although we start and stop reading at will, although we initiate, continue, and end our entire encounter with a book, when the game into which we are invited is being played, we are the book's plaything, its mouth, its mind, its motion, there to be done with what it likes. Few things are better than learning of one's own range at the hands of a skilled player, a delight described by Emily Dickinson:

> My Life had stood—a Loaded Gun
> In Corners—till a Day
> The Owner passed—identified—
> And carried Me away—
>
> And now We roam in Sovereign Woods—
> And now We hunt the Doe—
> And every time I speak for Him
> The Mountains straight reply—

That this play is a perennial surprise is the most joyful part of it. Setting oneself against it is easy enough, but no amount of willing it to happen will make it so. We can pursue the experience of being taken over by a book as monomaniacally as we like and it will still take us unawares, still somehow happen when we least expect it. The psychoanalyst Christopher Bollas proposes:

Certain objects, like psychic "keys," open doors to unconsciously intense—and rich—experience in which we articulate the self that we are through the elaborating character of our response. This selection constitutes the *jouissance* of the true self, a bliss released through the finding of specific objects that free idiom to its articulation.

"Selection" and "finding" shade into one another in that last sentence, a conjunction that is worth some attention. *Selection* implies choice, something that we make happen. *Finding* happens to us. We may select many things without finding what we are looking for; we may look for many things and find many others. We may be found. Any necessary connection between selection and finding is, essentially, a matter of faith: "seek, and ye shall find." Bollas's psychoanalysis is rich in such faith: "No contribution to solving a scientific problem, to the final product of a poem, or to the designing of a car engine is lost on the unconscious." According to Bollas, in the realm of the Freudian unconscious we are all, without the trouble of trying, Henry James's "people on whom nothing is lost." "Trying," in fact, is not only unnecessary, but inimical to the "*jouissance* of the true self": "We dream ourself into being by using objects to stimulate our idiom, to release it into lived expression. We do not think about it at all while doing it." Who are we when we read, blissed-out subjects merged with objects, beside ourselves, and yet also inhabiting a particular, unreproducible idiom "freed" to its articulation? We are, Bollas suggests, truly and strangely ourselves, less discrete than we ordinarily are:

> The distinction between the subject who uses the object to fulfill his desire and the subject who is played upon by the action of the object is no longer possible.

When Bollas speaks of individuals and the objects they use, he means aesthetic objects, like books and music, but he means all other objects of our attention as well: the food we eat, the people we know, the places we live, the jobs we do. His subject is the human self, and he makes no claims for any one means to rich inner experience over another. Nevertheless, he is drawn to examples of people losing and finding themselves in books and music, because aesthetic experience so vividly concentrates the paradoxes of self-making and self-unmaking, the play of present and not present, same and changed, that he sees at the heart of all psychic work. Above all, our capacity to lose ourselves in a piece of art highlights the freedom of choice that has to be present if a self is to come into being and stay open to its own becoming. Limitations are the essence of games, but freedom of participation, which means freedom of assent to those limitations, is the essence of play. As Carse has it, "Whoever *must* play cannot *play*."

At the same time, Carse's vision of play, "to allow for possibility whatever the cost to oneself," is an ideal, one few of us can always live up to, because, like the "*jouissance*" of the "true self" as Bollas imagines it, it may involve suffering. It is guaranteed to be exhausting. Playing means choosing to lay down "that weapon, self-protectiveness," and it is rare to be drawn readily to being unprotected. For one thing, it precludes the possibility of feeling like a winner. Winning needs finished games and it needs losers; its signs are titles, property, and power. The title *winner* "effectively takes a person out of play," and there are always reasons to want to be out of play. Play is unsettled, unfinished, in motion. While we are in play, we are equal with all other players, all decisions are still in abeyance, all outcomes possible. When such uncertainty feels unbearable there are many ways to foreclose it. Bollas writes:

Self experiencing cannot be assumed. Some individuals . . .
insist that the invitational feature of the object be declined. . . .
They may narrow the choice of objects, eliminating those with a
high evocative potential.

Seen in this light, the choice by readers no longer to read is
an expression of a positive wish to remain composed and fixed.
Bollas says there are "some individuals" who feel this reluctance,
but surely it is more accurate to say there is this reluctance in every individual, to greater or lesser degree, at different times in his
or her life. Reading, like most of the uses of this world, can feel
weary, stale, flat, and unprofitable.

Or perhaps it is more accurate to say that boredom can over-
whelm even reading's rewards. Boredom, play's opposite, begins
with a "no." It is a refusal of the moment at hand, a denial of
one's presence in that moment. Boredom is a protest against the
present, a profound form of negation, the antithesis of acceptance. To accept what is (which does not mean to like it) is to
continue to play with it, even if that play involves doing nothing
at all. Bartleby the Scrivener, preferring not to play the game as
it is understood by the people around him, is not bored. Boredom's pain, so intolerable for children, is the sign of a silence on
the other end of a psychic line. Our being is a call that wants an
answer, a shout that demands not an echo, "its own love back in
copy speech, / But counter-love, original response." When nothing answers us, when nothing seems capable of answering us,
we are bored. In this way boredom commonly involves resent-
ment, anxiety, loneliness, anger, and any number of other active
feeling-states. When we become habitual shouters, and allow
our capacity for listening to atrophy, we enter the worst of all
worlds, boredom fed by fury: "'Love should be put into action!' /

screamed the old hermit. / Across the pond an echo / tried and tried to confirm it."

A child, "a new beginning, a game, a wheel rolling out of itself, a first movement, a sacred yes-saying," will do nearly anything to escape boredom and return to play. Adults may have a more ambivalent relationship to their own boredom, especially since boredom can appear seductively like rest. Boredom is a temptation. Play is hopefulness, caring, an investment in what happens next without the power or wish to control what happens next. Play is risk, and a surrender to activity and pursuit. The mind under threat, in an attitude of defense or aggression, or the fatigued mind, sees only the exposure play requires, as well as the letting go of a sense of justice. Play goes on and on. No one wins or loses while it continues. Nothing is decided. To a contracted mind, freedom feels like a sting, like a sleeping limb starting to wake up. Allowing the flow and inrush of feeling, to a certain temperament, after a certain period of stasis, might seem too painful.

In this kind of state, the speaker of Elizabeth Bishop's poem "The End of March" takes a walk on the beach with a friend, through a gray and "indrawn" landscape, where "everything was withdrawn as far as possible." In the course of their walk they encounter puzzles without solutions, enigmas without point: dog-prints the size of lion-prints, "lengths and lengths, endless, of wet white string, / looping up to the tide-line, down to the water," and at the end of that string a huge snarl, "man-size." They pause long enough to speculate that the string might once have been a "kite string?" but concede immediately that they find "no kite." Puzzles, for the curious, are games. Stray objects set together by chance allow, to the playful mind, the possibility of design, order, intention, meaning. In another, less frozen inner landscape, such an array of objects would constitute an invitation to wide imagining. Ruthie, the narrator of Marilynne Robinson's *Housekeeping*, describes the course such imagining might take in a mind, like a child's, not set against it:

> My grandmother had kept, in the bottom drawer of the chest of drawers, a collection of things, memorabilia, balls of twine, Christmas candles, and odd socks. Lucille and I used to delve in this drawer. Its contents were so randomly assorted, yet so neatly arranged, that we felt some large significance might be behind the collection as a whole.

As she looks at the objects in their mysterious array, Ruthie thinks of her evangelist aunt Molly, whom she has never met, becoming a "fisher of men." In Ruthie's mind, Molly floats in the "spumy billows of the upper air" with a net that would

> pull . . . in a pell-mell ascension of formal gentlemen and thin pigs and old women and odd socks that would astonish this lower world. . . . One last pull of measureless power and ease would spill her catch into the boat, gasping and amazed, gleaming rainbows in the rarer light.
>
> Such a net, such a harvesting, would put an end to all anomaly.

Robinson's image of the rainbow-gleaming catch, beyond "all anomaly," itself calls back to Bishop's poem "The Fish." In that poem, the eponymous fish looks to the narrator's probing, minutely attentive gaze like a collection of oddly assorted things, with skin like wallpaper, eye like foil, unseen swim-bladder like a peony, and old, embedded fishing hooks like "medals with their ribbons / frayed" or a "beard of wisdom." The poet is immersed in her looking, playing with, reading, each part of the fish as it comes before her eyes, "without any irritable reaching after fact and reason," when suddenly the fish, in its coherence, power, serenity, age, and persistence, is present to her whole. This "victory," of the poet's attention and the fish's wholeness, "fill[s] up / the little rented boat, / . . . until everything / [is] rainbow, rainbow, rainbow!" So complete is that victorious catch, in which poet has caught fish and fish has caught poet, so apart from the world of trophies is it, that the speaker "let[s] the fish go." While the poet's eye plays over the fish and her mind moves freely among its seemingly unrelated associations, an inner whole is restored.

For Robinson's Ruthie, reeling from the successive losses of people who might have made her child's world cohere (mother, grandmother, aunts, and sister soon enough), the restoration of wholeness seems possible only from a world beyond her own, by someone riding the "spumy billows" of a different plane. Back on her cold beach, meanwhile, Bishop's brooding poet is disinclined to make the world whole again herself. She turns away from the imaginative game presented by those lion-size dogprints and man-size string-snarl out of what looks less like despair or mourning than simple fatigue. Choosing not to play, she faces inward, turning away from her wandering in the present and toward a fixed destination, a mysterious and ramshackle house farther down the beach. Struggling into the icy cold wind, she pictures it, jerry-rigged and absurd-looking, "a sort of artichoke of a house," in which she will be sheltered from the need to read and interpret the world's mysteries. She thinks of that house, described though never actually seen in the poem, as her "proto-dream-house," her "crypto-dream-house," a place that is the first and the last, the beginning and the end, a bare sketch of a house, encrypted against detection. Once there, she will do "*nothing*, / or nothing much," which means, tellingly, reading "boring books / old, long, long books" about which she will write "useless notes." This reading will not change her. She will take it in and feel nothing, be roused to no response, give nothing back, play with no one.

It's a restful fantasy for a writer. Elsewhere, in "Crusoe in England," Bishop dramatizes the plight of the poet by imagining herself as Crusoe, stranded on an island with nothing but the patchy memory of what he has read to give him human company. Like any habitual reader, he is tormented by the blanks in his recall. When he is eventually rescued, "one of the first things" he does is look up a line of Wordsworth he couldn't remember. (Ironically, the word that eludes him on the island is *solitude*.) Even worse are his nightmares, in which his poetic vocation, his calling to respond to the world, becomes, in the absence of other minds with which to share it, consumingly repetitive. "I'd have / nightmares of other islands," he says,

> stretching away from mine, infinities
> of islands, islands spawning islands,
> . . . knowing that I had to live
> on each and every one, eventually,
> for ages, registering their flora,
> their fauna, their geography.

In the imaginary dream house of "The End of March," by contrast, no such problems exist. There are no nagging holes in the reader's memory. The books are not memorable, and even if they were, they are all there to be consulted. There are no new lands to explore, no troublesome changes to account for. Activity itself continues (words are processed, alcohol is drunk), but play, the openness of possibility, ceases.

The poet is fantasizing about death. What else could the free choice to read "boring" books be? Reading books that *other people* find boring is not the issue. Ravenous readers do that all the time, looking up only every now and then to wonder vaguely how anyone could be bored by them. The choice to read what is boring to oneself, however, which nearly always involves suppressing the knowledge that one is in fact bored, is a kind of suicide of the mind, a refusal to visit the wellspring of one's own voice. To read boring books forever is the equivalent of joining Emily Dickinson on her Death-driven carriage ride to "a House that seemed / A Swelling of the Ground" where all the poem can do is "pause" for centuries, forever, caught in a time for which human language has no terms, in which it is no longer at play. The "crypto-dream-house" is also a crypt in which the poet's life and work are laid to rest. While there, Bishop's speaker chooses against any possibility of loss or learning or love. The world of the beach house is comprehensible and whole, but only because it is so grievously, so inhumanly contracted. It is no place to sit and read.

Poetically speaking, the beach is often a dividing line between shelter, civilization, domesticity, order, and life (the land), and possibility, violence, exploration, chaos, and death (the sea). It is where poets go to have a foot in both worlds, to pledge their allegiance to borders rather than nations, to test the strength of their voice against that of the "inhuman . . . veritable ocean." Death is an intimate, beckoning presence on the shore. It is what draws poets there, inviting them to "put away [their] labor and [their] leisure too" and be merged with something bigger and more powerful than they are. Hearing this invitation clearly, feeling and articulating the full force of its pull, and then living to tell about it, is one way poets win their right to be called "poet." Walt Whitman wrote one of his greatest poems about such a moment, when the child he was, playing on the Long Island shore, receives his vocation from the voice of the sea itself:

> A word then, (for I will conquer it,)
> The word final, superior to all,
> Subtle, sent up—what is it?—I listen;
> Are you whispering it, and have been all the time, you
> sea-waves?
> Is that it from your liquid rims and wet sands?

> Whereto answering, the sea,
> Delaying not, hurrying not,
> Whisper'd me through the night, and very plainly
> before daybreak,
> Lisp'd to me the low and delicious word death.

Emily Dickinson wins the sea's notice by absorbing as much of its power as she can before turning back at the last moment:

> But no Man moved Me—till the Tide
> Went past my simple Shoe—
> And past my Apron—and my Belt
> And past my Boddice—too—

> And made as He would eat me up—
> As wholly as a Dew

Opon a Dandelion's Sleeve—
And then—I started—too—

. . .

And bowing with a Mighty look—
At me—The Sea withdrew—

Marianne Moore, more cautious than either Whitman or Dickinson, nevertheless feels the ocean's unchanged power and danger:

Man looking into the sea,
taking the view from those who have as much right to
    it as you have to it yourself,
it is human nature to stand in the middle of a thing
but you cannot stand in the middle of this:
the sea has nothing to give but a well excavated grave.

As these poets, and countless others, bear witness, the shore is a powerful place for a poet to visit, but an impossible place to live. In Carse's terms, Bishop's residence in a house by the sea, where all games are at an end and only boring books are read, would relieve her of the considerable burden of being an "infinite speaker," whose "speech has the form of listening." He calls such speakers "storytellers," in whose speaking "we begin to see the narrative character of our lives. . . . What we thought was an accidental sequence of experience suddenly takes the dramatic shape of unresolved narrative." When Bishop accedes to the impossibility of reaching her imaginary house ("the wind was much too cold / even to get that far"), with its seductive (and terrible) promise to end her life as a storyteller, and turns back to face the world and its call to be heard and read and told, she is rewarded:

> The sun came out for just a minute.
> For just a minute, set in their bezels of sand,
> the drab, damp, scattered stones
> were multi-colored,
> and all those high enough threw out long shadows,
> individual shadows, then pulled them in again.
> They could have been teasing the lion sun,
> except that now he was behind them
> —a sun who'd walked the beach the last low tide,
> making those big, majestic paw-prints,
> who perhaps had batted a kite out of the sky to play with.

Having dwelled imaginatively in her "dream-house" long enough to feel fully the pull of its charm, and having chosen nevertheless to return to her life as a poet, the speaker is able, without any apparent effort, to restore the seemingly "accidental sequence" of objects on her beach walk into a powerful narrative whole. The dog was a lion, and the lion was the sun, and there *was* a kite, which was destroyed in an encounter with that supreme force. What she encountered was not meaningless and fragmentary, in other words, but told a story (those lengths and lengths of string, looping up and down, turn out to have been a sort of writing), waiting to reach the right reader.

Reading is picking up a line and following it, feeling that all lines, like the limp leash of a cord behind Bishop's beach house, run to and from a power source, "something off behind the dunes." We will never reach that source. It is dangerous even to approach it, because it asks of us ways of being for which we are not built. Bishop's return to the world of playful reading, which is colorful and expressive, and in which all the elements form a story, bears traces of the lethal forces just outside of her (and our) playful consciousness. The lion sun is equally life-giver and predator, the source of all life on land and sea who is yet destructive even in his lightest play—the kite does not survive its encounter with him. Nor would Bishop have. Her imaginative success, which is to say her imaginative survival, depends on the circuitousness with which she reenters the world as a place to play. Having refused the refuge of boring books, she is welcomed back into a world where everything is to be read, and hence where everything is at stake. She reenters the world of her poem as part of literature, where the most important work gets done offstage, behind our own backs, somewhere sequestered from our direct attention and pursuit for our own protection.

III

◆

Transgression

To transgress is to step across a boundary. No intention, no plan, no consciousness is necessary for transgression to take place. All that are necessary are an imaginary line and someone to cross it. Transgression's close relative and manifestation in the physical world, trespass, demonstrates why transgression is a crime. Trespassing on another's property is an offense against the idea of property itself. When I step onto your land without permission, I have refused to acknowledge your title to that land. My challenge is to you, personally, and to the entire system of entitlements and their enforcement in which you participate. My existence on the wrong side of a boundary is enough to set in motion such a challenge. Nothing I do there makes any difference; cultivating another's land is as bad as poisoning it when the idea of property is at stake. The laws of property define what I am ("trespasser") according to where I am, not according to what I do, think, say, believe, intend, or hope while I am there. My presence there affects everyone with a stake in the wider system, on whatever side of whatever boundary they happen to be. Sometimes it's the boundaries that move. If those with power redraw a line while I sleep, I awake a trespasser without ever having taken a step.

Boundary lines are no less powerful for being hard to locate precisely, and nearly impossible to fix permanently. Looking for a boundary, one more often finds zones rather than lines, sites where meanings are unfixed, populated by people in transition, temporarily or permanently outside the prevailing order. Some such zones may be physical (the crossroads, the marketplace, borderlands) but more are not. The half-worlds of letters, phone calls, and electronic messages of all kinds are especially effective at bringing people to and across boundaries. Night, of course, is the most propitious time to transgress.

Literary objects "press back against the pressure of reality" by declining to respect otherwise useful demarcations. Such as: between subjective and objective, possible and impossible, dead and alive. To the extent that it presses back most vigorously in this way, poetry is the most essentially literary art, and the place to look for the finest record of our private travels across dividing lines. A dialogue between two poems, by Robert Frost and Thylias Moss, presents in microcosm the elements of transgression involved in reading. Frost's 1923 poem "Stopping by Woods on a Snowy Evening" concisely illustrates the drama, however silent and internal, of transgression that takes place when an individual mind considers the world around it. The poem begins,

> Whose woods these are I think I know.
> His house is in the village though;
> He will not see me stopping here
> To watch his woods fill up with snow.

Frost's narrator, the speaking "I" of the poem, is an interloper, a man looking on another man's property and so already engaged in challenging property rights. Those rights are held by the woods' owner, who lives "in the village," which is to say, in the stronghold of domesticity, an area defined by being cordoned off from the wilderness. Ensconced in domesticity, that owner will not see Frost's narrator stopping to watch the woods, hidden as the narrator is by the darkness and the cold, elements against which the village is designed to defend. Therefore, although there is trespass taking place, there will be no immediate contest and the interloper's challenge will go unanswered.

Which is not to say that the interloping narrator himself does not have a good bit of village nature in him. In the final stanza of the poem, famously, he turns away from the wild woods:

> The woods are lovely, dark and deep,
> But I have promises to keep,
> And miles to go before I sleep,
> And miles to go before I sleep.

In the end, the narrator is called away from his transgressive musing by "promises," forays into property's future, that require him to travel distances measurable in miles. He will not stay to "sleep" (a state in which promises have little claim on us). Even his challenge to the laws of ownership suggests his easy familiarity with them; it is his security within them that licenses his brief dalliance away from them. He is white; he is male; he rides alone at night without fear.

Or maybe the "I" of the poem is none of those things. When we say "I" we refer by definition to ourselves alone. When you read "I," "the only voice [you hear] is your own." Not the voice as others hear it, but the one only we ourselves will ever know, without sound, and without ordinary limit. Reading is a state of voice in which others speak through us, and in which others come to us only when their voices and ours are indistinguishable. There is wide latitude for interpenetration in that state, a lifting of boundaries otherwise vigilantly patrolled, a wandering between and among that, if it took place anywhere else, would constitute transgression of the most chaotic kind. A cat may look at a king. Readers are cats and kings simultaneously.

When Frost is read by the poet Thylias Moss, as in her poem "Interpretation of a Poem by Frost," the pronoun "I" who speaks it takes on new shadings. Her "interpretation" of Frost makes new sense of his poem, word by word. It is as though she is reading it in Braille, bringing to bear an entirely new sensory apparatus on it. The uncanniness of Moss's "Interpretation" of Frost arises from the radical naïveté of its premise: that "I" refers to the person who reads rather than the person who writes. "A young black girl stopped by the woods," she begins,

> so young she knew only one man: Jim Crow
> but she wasn't allowed to call him Mister.
> The woods were his and she respected his boundaries
> even in the absence of fence.
> Of course she delighted in the filling up
> of his woods, she so accustomed to emptiness,
> to being taken at face value.

Moss's poem (one of many possible interpretations) about what happens when she and Frost say "I" together is also a story about reading as a counterforce to the laws of property. What is yours is mine when I read you. What is you is me when I read you. In reading "I," I "effuse my flesh in eddies, and drift it in lacy jags." "I" slip the bonds of self and see what happens. Some things are the same when Moss reads "Stopping by Woods on a

Snowy Evening": boundaries and trespass are still at issue. The "I" of the poem does not need fences to know just where the boundaries are and bears them continually in mind. It is still the case that an owner need not to be present in order for his rights to be firmly asserted. In both poems, too, the mere act of looking is a challenge to those rights.

There are differences, though. The owner of the woods Moss's girl stops by does not live in any one house or village. "Jim Crow" is an idea, a title, the legal (which is to say fictive yet real) foundation of all the houses, and villages, and woods among which she lives. She is forbidden to address him—to presume even the deferential relationship greetings imply. She knows who he is, but she does not know him the way Frost's rider may know his unseen rival for ownership of the woods. What she sees is different, too, the fullness and whiteness of the snow taking on particular meaning for an underestimated Black girl already alive to the rules of her world. She, with a

> face eternally the brown
> of declining autumn, watches snow inter the grass,
> cling to bark making it seem indecisive
> about race preference, a fast-to-melt idealism.

The woods are lovely to Moss's girl because they are a place where black and white "cling" as they do nowhere in her human world. She knows too much to stay in them, though, having had experience of that transient idealism, so "the snow does not hypnotize her as it wants to" and she turns away. Like Frost before her, she is headed back to face the promises she has yet to keep. Unlike him, she enumerates the promises, some of them impossible for her to keep alone, into which she was born:

the promise that she bear Jim no bastards,
the promise that she ride the horse only as long
as it is willing to accept riders,
the promise that she bear Jim no bastards,
the promise to her face that it not be mistaken as
    shadow.

No one person could keep such promises. The promise not to bear bastards, for example, requires a woman not to have a child, and therefore a man who does not impregnate her, or that she bear a child, in a realm of men who make laws under which her child is "legitimate." She may be able not to mistake her own face as shadow, but she would have to be all people everywhere to ensure that it is never so mistaken by others. She would have to be many people simultaneously.

Who is Thylias Moss? The testimony of her poems is varied and contradictory. She is a permanent eighth grader with a friend named Molly wondering impishly, "What are we doing in your mouth?" Her ancestry is "dense." She is a dog, "sometimes," with "vestiges of . . . evolution giving [her] dreams, instincts, secrets for dark / recall." She is more than what she wears, "no polyester, no rayon or / charmeuse blouse [her] creator," but she arose from a "pit of crinoline ruffles." No "long Caucasian history served / in a smorgasbord of texts" was meant to "sustain" her, but she was born with "a piece of Galileo's brain," a "common woman," with a "common problem": "her flesh, so excessive / at all the creases," masking the "faithful, uncompromising truthful bone" beneath.

Was Moss a young Black girl when she read Frost's poem? On the page that faces her "Interpretation of a Poem by Robert Frost" is a poem called "The Lynching." The latter poem doesn't announce itself as, but is, an interpretation of Claude McKay's

"The Lynching." McKay's poem, about a lynched body, a "swinging char," ends with a premonition of further violence perpetuated endlessly by the watching crowd's "little lads, lynchers that were to be," dancing "round the dreadful thing in fiendish glee." The speaker of Moss's poem, the voice that says "I" when Moss writes it, is one of those lads, though he is not gleeful. McKay's poem describes the lynched man's having been called home to his heavenly "father," by "cruelest way of pain." Moss's narrator counters with a child's certainty that "No parent // of atrocity is in heaven." He thinks instead about his own father, one of the lynchers, who "baptizes by fire same as / Jesus will"; "becomes a holy ghost when / he dons his sheet." In McKay's poem the hanging body is watched over during the night by a single "pitiful" star. In Moss's, the son of a father in whom "the God . . . / does not glow" sleeps under the incinerated body, "[its] thin moon-begot / shadow as mattress," becoming joined to it:

> something smoldering
> keeps me warm. Patches of skin fall onto me
> in places I didn't know needed mending.

This white child, patched and made whole by falling flakes of burned black skin, is a kind of monster. To be specific, he is a peculiarly American incarnation of Frankenstein's monster, the product of many-faceted miscegenation: an unlawful mixture of white and black, living and dead, adult and child, earthly and airborne. He is made in the out-of-bounds places that will also be where he can be seen and tolerated: at night, in sleep, outdoors. And in Thylias Moss's mind as she read, and in ours as we read.

The white child patched with burned black skin is a monster made of words. Moss conjured him into being with words, and his monstrosity consists of bringing together categorical differences that are only different as long as we agree on words that keep them that way. "Black" skin is rarely black; "white" skin is rarely white. Transgression exists where there is a language to assert separation and fixity in the face of what otherwise moves, merges, and mutates ceaselessly. The real world is famously amenable to combinations that violate categories some prefer to remain immutable. The human genome, for example, has no words for *black* or *white*, so "the mind cheats, soft / and dreaming, inventing words bone can't say, not even a simple / forensics-defying word: race." But then, even as words name and make real our fears, enact our "rage for order," they are also channels of exchange running between us. They are pathways for the introduction of a kind of genetic diversity of the imagination on which psychic health (if not comfort or happiness) depends. We read to tend what was and must remain wild within us, "to locate those zones inside us that would be free and declare them so," whatever the cost.

◆

In Hesiod's *Theogony*, Prometheus, seeing humankind cold and miserable, brings us fire. Fire, the "inexhaustible," had specifically been withheld from mortals by Zeus, making Prometheus's gift one that has implicated humankind ever since in a transgression against our own divinely ordained limitations. From this unstable, unpredictable, flickering gift all of our strength, our culture, our knowledge follows. Its heat is what we carry inside, the essential thing we pass to and receive from others: "ardor comes before thought. Thoughts are given off like steam from a boiling liquid." Fire is heat, and it is also light in the darkness. The human mastery of fire angers the gods who see it "twinkle . . . from afar," because light is inextricable from knowledge. Light under human control frees us to pursue knowledge at unnatural hours, which leads inevitably to pursuing unnatural knowledge. From Quixote reading "from dusk till dawn" by candlelight, to a present-day child under her covers reading on a smartphone, "the real literary experience" is transgressive, and depends on Prometheus's illicit gift.

Reading is at the heart of the most resonant retelling of Prometheus's crime and punishment, Mary Shelley's *Frankenstein; or, The Modern Prometheus*. Victor Frankenstein, the maddened scientist who animates a stitched-together corpse, is the first candidate for the "modern Prometheus" of the book's subtitle. His crime, like Prometheus's, is trespassing on divine ground by stealing for himself knowledge withheld from mortals. After years of fevered reading in disreputable, forbidden books, he describes a gift of fire: "a sudden light broke in upon me," he says; "I succeeded in discovering the cause of generation and life; nay, more, I became myself capable of bestowing animation upon lifeless matter." He is cagey about the specifics of this illumination, because, he explains, the punishments that followed it were so severe. "I will not lead you on," he tells his interlocutor and, by extension, his reader, "unguarded and ardent as I then was, to your destruction and infallible misery. Learn from me, if not by my precepts, at least by my example, how dangerous is the acquirement of knowledge."

Frankenstein's punishments are doled out by the Creature he makes, the living embodiment of the knowledge he regrets having acquired. Before he is through, the Creature murders Frankenstein's younger brother, best friend, and foster sister/fiancée, each a paragon in his or her own way. Seen in this light, the Creature is the serpent in the garden, bent on the destruction of the Rousseauvian childhood Eden in which Frankenstein was educated:

> Our studies were never forced; and by some means we always had an end placed in view, which excited us to ardour in the prosecution of them. It was by this method, and not by emulation, that we were urged to application.
>
> . . .
>
> Neither of us possessed the slightest pre-eminence over the other; the voice of command was never heard amongst us; but mutual affection engaged us all to comply with and obey the slightest desire of each other.

Seen in another light, Frankenstein's Creature, product of his hands and flower of his learning, is Frankenstein's liberator, doing what Victor himself cannot: eradicating the demands of domestic life by destroying those who embody them. Frankenstein himself speaks piously of limitations, urging abstinence from "unlawful" study that "weakens your affections and . . . destroy[s] your taste for those simple pleasures in which no alloy can possibly mix." His Creature, meanwhile, powerful beyond containment, has no check on his feelings, and no inhibition in their expression. He is alloyed all through, his adoration mixed with hatred, erudition permeating his elemental existence.

Victor Frankenstein is one model of Prometheus, stealing fire under the name of "the cause of generation and life." His Creature, however, is another, and it is his story of transgression and punishment that echoes in the mind of the reader. This is because the Creature's crime is reading itself. He steals literacy, the spark of his nascent self-consciousness, from a world designed to keep it from him. His theft leads him to knowledge of himself, a poisoned gift that bestows a soul and the suffering that goes with it. Both creator and Creature are "ruined by reading," though it is hard to say exactly what is wrong with Frankenstein's reading. It is untutored, and it awakens fantasies of "unlawful" power that persist even when his formal education begins and he no longer believes in outmoded scientific doctrines. Perhaps he does too much of it. But none of this would seem so bad without the deus ex machina that descends to hand over, behind a modesty screen of his discretion on the subject, "the cause of generation." Few readers have to worry about this kind of thing. Godlike power, for better or for worse, is not the usual outcome of too much unsupervised reading. The Creature's reading is another story altogether, because it bestows only, but exactly, the power and pain of self-knowledge. His circumstances may be unusually heightened, but his problem is not: because he reads, he knows more than he wants to, and he knows it too well to forget it. If Victor Frankenstein is a "modern" Prometheus, a transgressive thief born of the science of his age, his Creature is both a modern and an ancient one, repeating a crime as old as Eden and suffering the same punishment: an understanding of himself and of his origins. His story is the one of which lifelong readers live out endless variations.

Why do popular reimaginings of the Frankenstein story in the movies omit his literacy? It's a striking change from the novel, in which the essence of Shelley's creature is that he can argue his case. In Shelley's vision, the Creature is his creator's match in learning and eloquence, superior in wits as well as physical strength to the human world that hates him on sight. One answer is that literacy turns monsters, which are frightening, chaotic, and destructive, into villains, who may be all of those things but are also, inevitably, seductive. A monster and a villain both might kill you, but a villain may convert you to his cause first.

A villain is usually just a step away from being a story's hero. A monster's muteness can also evoke our pity, allowing us, in conquering it, the possibility of a double victory: defeating a monster eliminates an external threat, while pitying it restores our internal sense of power that fear takes away. Monsters can be made into pets—villains cannot. Frankenstein's Creature, in the grunting, illiterate form the movies have given him, is less menacing to our egotism than the creature Shelley imagined. Once that creature can tell his own story—once he knows himself as having a story to tell—he is lost to us as a pure object of pity or terror. He is a self without reference to us at all.

For Shelley's Creature, then, the transgression against the man who made him, as well as against boundaries that divide the human from the nonhuman, is not reading one book or another; it is reading at all. Victor Frankenstein's inaugural act of fatherhood is to reject the newly animated Creature's first words by running out of the room. Quick to take the hint, the Creature flees to the woods, where he lives alone, learning the uses of his own senses, discovering fire, and eventually finding a family from whom he can learn to be human. That education centers on literacy, which he pursues by means of eavesdropping, listening in as the family teaches French to a young woman in their care. He first learns to follow their spoken language and then, cataclysmically, to read. As the Creature learns "the science of letters," they initially "open before [him] a wide field for wonder and delight." As he becomes proficient in reading, however, the words "turn him toward himself," and he falls irrevocably into self-consciousness. Like Adam and Eve before him, the creature comes away from his encounter with the tree of knowledge with a fatal question: "What was I?" He arrives at much the same answer: naked and ashamed. The crime of knowledge, which for

74

the Creature is the crime of reading, is its own punishment, as he learns to his cost: "Of what a strange nature is knowledge! It clings to the mind, when it has once seized on it, like a lichen on the rock."

◆

In learning to read, Frankenstein's monster learns the exhilarations and desolations of freedom. He is emancipated from ignorance of himself and his condition—freed to confront the full measure of his enslavement. The story is an old one, and also an ever-new one: Maggie Verver has a vision of her marriage as an elaborate pagoda into which she can find no entrance; Don Gately realizes he lives at the mercy of "the planet's most remorselessly hard-ass and efficient sergeant at arms"; Neo wakes up from the Matrix. Jill Lepore reports that for the abolitionist-minded Mary Shelley the story of the Creature's liberation from bondage had immediate connections to contemporary British debates about the nation's continued profit from slave-run industries in its territories. Shelley's reading public was alert to those connections, adopting the Creature as an emblem on both sides of the debate. For abolitionists, he was a symbol of the slave arguing his just case for freedom. For defenders of slavery, his powerful body and murderous rage concretized their beliefs that enslaved African people were innately savage and so unfit for citizenship.

Few readers have been better positioned to gauge the truth of Shelley's fable of literacy and self-knowledge than Frederick Douglass, a man born into slavery who made himself into one of his age's greatest orators on the nature of freedom. On the evidence of his *Narrative of the Life*, we can infer Douglass's deep receptiveness both to the meaning of the Creature's struggle for and with self-knowledge, and to Shelley's description of it. Douglass was a keen, lifelong reader and reciter of Romantic poetry. The reverberations of Shelley's rhetoric can be heard in a pivotal scene in the *Narrative*, in which Douglass describes how he learned to read and what the consequences of that knowledge were. Like Shelley's Creature, Douglass is a thief of reading. He learns it by turning "the little white boys whom [he] met in the street" (not yet sufficiently trained by slave culture to safeguard literacy against interlopers) into teachers. He gives them bread, and they give him lessons in reading the books he carries with him for the purpose while running errands. Having thus transgressed, Douglass is simultaneously rewarded and punished by what he finds in the world of books. Like the Creature before him, Douglass is transformed by his encounter with eighteenth-century rhetoric. The Creature learns from Volney's *Ruins of Empires* "the strange system of human society" with its "division of property . . . rank, descent, and noble blood," while the twelve-year-old Douglass learns from *The Columbian Orator* "the power of truth over the conscience of even a slaveholder."

Though he does not say so, Douglass also took from *Frankenstein* itself the language with which to represent his painful experience of reading and the self-knowledge it brings him. The Creature, having learned from his reading to know his own condition, describes his suffering this way:

> Of my creation and creator I was absolutely ignorant; but I knew that I possessed no money, no friends, no kind of property. . . . When I looked around, I saw and heard of none like me. Was I then a monster, a blot upon the earth, from which all men fled, and whom all men disowned?
>
> I cannot describe to you the agony that these reflections

inflicted upon me; I tried to dispel them, but sorrow only increased with knowledge. Oh, that I had for ever remained in my native wood, nor known nor felt beyond the sensations of hunger, thirst, and heat!

Of what a strange nature is knowledge! It clings to the mind, when once it has seized on it, like a lichen on the rock. I wished sometimes to shake off all thought and feeling; but I learned that there was but one means to overcome the sensation of pain, and that was death—a state which I feared yet did not understand.

Like the Creature, Douglass was also raised to be "absolutely ignorant" of his creation and creator, as the opening paragraph of his *Narrative* attests. "By far the larger part of the slaves know as little of their ages as horses know of theirs," he notes, with brutal flatness. "Of my father," he continues, "I know nothing; the means of knowing was withheld from me." When knowledge of himself does dawn, his language closely mirrors Shelley's Creature's:

As I read and contemplated the subject, behold! that very discontentment which Master Hugh had predicted would follow my learning to read had already come, to torment and sting my soul to unutterable anguish. As I writhed under it, I would at times feel that learning to read had been a curse rather than a blessing. It had given me a view of my wretched condition, without the remedy. It opened my eyes to the horrible pit, but to no ladder upon which to get out. In moments of agony, I envied my fellow slaves for their stupidity. I have often wished myself a beast. I preferred the condition of the meanest reptile to my own. Anything, no matter what, to get rid of thinking! It was this everlasting thinking of my condition that tormented me. There was no getting rid of it.

. . .

I often found myself regretting my own existence, and wishing myself dead; and but for the hope of being free, I have no doubt but that I should have killed myself, or done something for which I should have been killed.

The scale of the crime committed against Douglass, and against the millions of enslaved people he represents, threatens to stop our own reading of his *Narrative* cold. In the face of the enormity of American slavery, it can seem irreverent to read the account of one who suffered it as anything but a kind of holy text, to absorb and be changed by. What place does the transgressive freedom, the wild pleasure, the painful inward-turning, of promiscuous reading, ours or Douglass's, have in such a story?

It has a necessary place. It is an aspect of exactly the freedom the slave system sought to deny its captives. Pruning our reading of the *Narrative* of any of its implications, including its enmeshment with fictional voices, is a way of refusing to respond to the rangy power of Douglass's writing. Such a refusal is, in its small, well-intentioned way, yet another infringement on the self-determination he insisted on as his right. It freezes him in the role of victim-paragon, denying the kinetic strength his of writing, that is born, like all writing that lasts, of the freely shifting self that reading grants. Reading requires that we stay "liquid," a state, in Terrance Hayes's words, "as much about uncertainty as it is about mutable sensibility: adaptive temperaments and temperatures and forms." Our fluid selves are at stake in reading, and "the idea of liquidness (fluidity? Liquidity?) is not limited by race or class, or gender—the more oppressed or disenfranchised one is, the more important one's liquidness." Douglass's story about learning to read and its consequences is itself a product of his reading. Having crossed the line into literacy, he has nowhere outside of it to stand while telling the story of that crossing, no words to tell it with that don't come saturated with their history of circulation through other eyes, mouths, and minds. The mind freed to wander in books is never again free of the consequences of that wandering. The mind so freed becomes largely constituted by that wandering, and capable as a result of breathtaking defiances of time, circumstance, and probability.

Douglass's story is a case in point. Shelley's Creature is in large part made of myth—equal parts Prometheus, Satan, and Adam—that came to Shelley by way of her own reading in the Bible, Milton, and elsewhere. All of these figures, writers and characters both, were part of the nineteen-year-old Mary Shelley, who made herself into the author of a Creature in which a formerly enslaved American memoirist and orator, not yet twenty-five, could find an image of himself that would help shape the lives of countless others in their own states of bondage. (Including Charlotte Brontë. Listen to the echoes of Douglass, "alone upon the lofty banks" of the Chesapeake Bay, "pour[ing] out [his] soul's complaint," when Jane Eyre "climb[s] . . . three staircases, raise[s] the trap-door of the attic," and "open[s her] inward ear to a tale that was never ended . . . quickened with all . . . that [she] desired and had not in [her] actual existence.") There is no essential distinction in this process between the fictional and the nonfictional. Douglass's enslavement was a fact, his chains literal, and his eventual liberation was a matter of planning, courage, and chance. But it was also a matter of reading, of entering a place without boundaries of age or color or condition, of logic or propriety or limit, and staying there long enough to be changed, and to change others. In reading, Shelley may look at Satan, and Satan at God, and the slave at his master, and the monster at his maker, and all of them may merge.

We have different names for this merging depending on our ethical judgments. From the perspective of his "owners," Douglass's reading, which is to say his entrance into imaginative freedom, was a civil crime and a violation of natural law. From ours it is an inspirational and reassuring fable about literacy as a vector of justice. In reading, however, it is not only the oppressed who can identify with and cross over into the territory of power—the paths run both ways, and those with more power also share in the worlds of those with less. When we feel hopeful, we call this empathy, but there are uglier names for this kind of crossing, too: appropriation, usurpation, imperialism. A certain kind of reader of Douglass's day was made uneasy, if not sickened and enraged, by the idea that literacy could make "white" experience available to Black minds. Many readers today are made uneasy by the reverse claim. The written work, as Plato warned, does not make distinctions among readers. All are invited into the worlds it opens, without qualification. The tension this creates, between the reader as citizen and the reader as reader, is real and biting.

Walt Whitman's poetry is uniquely at home in that uneasy territory between self and other, between civic and imaginative life. His poetry dwells there, probing the limits of our tolerance for the imaginative transformations in which reading traffics. Writing of the mother burned as a witch, and the runaway slave hounded by dogs and bullets, he says, "All this I swallow, it tastes good, I like it well, it becomes mine, / I am the man, I suffer'd, I was there." As a claim about real experience, his lines are an outrage; as a claim about reading, they are a commonplace. The question of what the difference between these two things is, and who gets to define it under what circumstances, cannot be settled. The transgressions inherent in reading do not follow easy or orderly ethical dividing lines. In reading we may lose the selves we are otherwise required to be, but we equally lose the selves we might prefer to be.

◆

We read to enter a place that is unpoliced and private, to step away from boundaries as we usually experience them. In this way, reading is a form of self-claiming. To the extent that our selves belong to others, it robs those others of their entitlement to us, so our reading is a self-theft, a crime in two senses. First, it asserts the existence of an independent self. Second, it removes that self from circulation, from its possible use as the property of others. The greater the claims a social system makes on an individual, the graver the transgression of reading will be. Where a threat to a system exists, volunteers will appear spontaneously to monitor and minimize it.

Jane Austen, the great anatomist of social systems and their enforcers, was alive to the special threat a devotion to reading posed to the social world in which she lived. Her well-known "defense of the novel" passage, in *Northanger Abbey*, is remembered as a refutation of prejudices against her chosen form, which, she notes tartly, unlike history, theology, or the daily news, "ha[s] only genius, wit, and taste to recommend [it]." The passage is about more than the novel, however. In it, Austen imagines the reaction of a young woman politely interrupted in her reading by a man:

"And what are you reading, Miss —?" "Oh! it is only a novel!" replies the young lady; while she lays down her book with affected indifference, or momentary shame.—"It is only *Cecilia*, or *Camilla*, or *Belinda*"; or, in short, only some work in which the greatest powers of the mind are displayed, in which the most thorough knowledge of human nature, the happiest delineation of its varieties, the liveliest effusions of wit and humour, are conveyed to the world in the best chosen language.

Had Miss — been reading *The Spectator*, Austen notes, "how proudly would she have produced the book, and told its name; though the chances must be against her being occupied by any part of that voluminous publication." Pointed as Austen's satire is on the subject of spurious literary judgments, Miss —'s situation is instructive in another direction. Irrespective of what she is reading, if she is doing it in public, Miss — will be interrupted by a curious gentleman. The interruption is what her public presence invites. Not to stop reading in the presence of male curiosity would be socially ruinous, but so would not appearing in public at all. Miss — is unlikely to have a room of her own (as her creator didn't). Without a study, without a space marked as off-limits to interruption, her reading must be done in the semi-public sphere of the drawing room. In that space her reading becomes, if it is not genuine reading, a performance of herself as a certain kind of young woman. If it is genuine, it becomes a transgression of the rules of young womanhood itself. Miss — has not been placed in a drawing room to negate the right of the gentlemen around her to her attention by absorbing herself in a book.

Reading's transgression against one's social enmeshments is resistant to compromise. It will not be bargained with. To read is to step outside the carefully patrolled boundaries of one's assigned sphere, and punishment is sure. A perennial strategy for outwitting this law is subterfuge. Perhaps, the hope goes, one will be able to read in the true sense under cover of reading because it is useful. Who could object to reading if it assists the maker of money in a household? allows one to know the gospel? prepares children for worldly success? enables one to improve the lives of others? makes better citizens? adorns the homemaker's loveliness? promotes empathy? teaches history? leads to a degree? results in the writing of a book? None of these are bad effects of reading, but they are ancillary to the discovery, assertion, and protection of freedom that lies at reading's core. That freedom will out.

Austen nimbly deploys her sketches of social skirmishes around reading behind an asbestos shield of satire. In *Middlemarch* her heir George Eliot develops Austen's theme into tragedy, focusing on those skirmishes and concentrating them into her portrait of a marital war over the stakes of a woman's reading. People, especially women who love to read, have been talking about *Middlemarch* since its publication. "'What do I think of *Middlemarch*?'" Emily Dickinson wrote her cousins in 1873, a year after its publication in one volume; "What do I think of glory—except that in a few instances this 'mortal has already put on immortality.'" Few figures from literature better illustrate the criminal ingenuity required to try to square reading's freedom with a life of constraint than Dorothea Brooke, the protagonist of *Middlemarch*. Dorothea is as book-crazed, in her way, as Don Quixote. Her books are different from his: she "knew many passages of Pascal's *Pensées* and Jeremy Taylor by heart," and like her spiritual forerunner Saint Teresa of Avila, she has no use for "many-volumed romances of chivalry." Nevertheless, her theological reading has unfitted her for the circumstances of her life, in which she is expected to have "weak opinions" that will not interfere with her husband's "political economy and the keeping of saddle-horses." Dorothea, maddened by her reading into imagining a life outside the bounds of her sex and her class, into imagining a self that might be larger than what those bounds can accommodate, rides into her future as haplessly as Quixote himself.

Eliot makes the parallel explicit in the second chapter, giving it an epigraph from Cervantes:

"Seest thou not yon cavalier who cometh toward us on a dapple-grey steed, and weareth a golden helmet?" "What I see," answered Sancho, "is nothing but a man on a grey ass like my own, who carries something shiny on his head." "Just so," answered Don Quixote: "and that resplendent object is the helmet of Mambrino."

In this chapter Dorothea, with her family, meets Mr. Casaubon, the elderly scholar who will shortly become her husband. No one else at that meeting imagines he might fill that role. While Dorothea is transfixed by the man of great learning and greater soul that her own needs have placed before her eyes, her sister Celia, younger, quieter, and considerably more grounded, eyes him with Sancho-like clarity:

When the two girls were in the drawing-room alone, Celia said—
"How very ugly Mr Casaubon is!"
"Celia! He is one of the most distinguished-looking men I ever saw. He is remarkably like the portrait of Locke. He has the same deep eye-sockets."
"Had Locke those two white moles with hairs on them?"

Eliot is alive to the comedy of Dorothea's particular mixture of intellectual power, worldly innocence, and unconscious moral arrogance. Her authorial attitude toward her creation in *Middle-march*'s early chapters is pity laced with gentle irony: "poor Doro-thea" is her most common epithet. Eliot is especially fond, which is also to say especially sharp, with respect to Dorothea's dream of finding a home for her freest self, a self given over to and merged with something infinite, in marriage to the right man. Dorothea, still a teenager, believes she has found a way to reconcile the size of her book-fueled spiritual ambition with the limited avenues available to her. All she needs is a "really delightful marriage" in which "your husband was a sort of father, and could teach you even Hebrew, if you wished it." Poor Dorothea.

An essential difference between Quixote's folly and Doro-thea's is that Quixote is male. His freedom to ride into trouble is never in doubt, and his punishments, gruesomely painful as some of them are, are comic. Quixote's freedom incites laughter. His transgressions against common sense and practical life make him simultaneously ludicrous and admirable. Having taken his lashes, suffered his broken bones, endured cold, hunger, and mockery, he is accepted easily back into the everyday world that loves him even while it cannot understand him. Dorothea, female, will have a harder time of it. Her transgression is tragic, a step out of bounds that leaves her changed, and exiled.

Dorothea is not the only character in the novel to learn hard lessons about the clash of reality with one's idealizations and fantasies. Lydgate, the arrogant young man who thinks that his devotion to higher thought will allow him to evade the traps of petty village politics, and that his superior education will give him the permanent upper hand with his wife, Rosamond, will end the novel broken. Rosamond herself has been denied the same education her brother Fred receives, and is the object of his mockery because of it. In fact, the only character to escape the novel unscathed is Mary Garth, Eliot's supreme portrait of an intelligent, sensitive, practical, ironic woman so well adjusted to life as to have no particular need of advanced learning or indeed of books at all. Mary Garth is so good that, ultimately, she does not need Eliot's attention. Rosamond is so stunted that Eliot is content to let her become the reality principle fettering Lydgate in a marriage of perfect incompatibility. Only Dorothea's story enters into the territory of myth, in which knowledge is forbidden, acquired in defiance of authority, and the subsequent bringer of both enlightenment and suffering.

Hide it though she does behind a screen of admirably feminine motives—principally, being of service to her scholar husband—Dorothea wants to taste forbidden fruit. She begs to learn Latin and Greek. Her alibi is that they will allow her to be more helpful to his great work, and she promises to learn to read them without understanding them. In reality, "those provinces of masculine knowledge seemed to her a standing-ground from which all truth could be seen more clearly." Mr. Casaubon colludes with her in her transgression: he teaches her to read the ancient languages. His alibi is that all he needs is better assistance, when the truth is that he can't do the work at all. He knows he is abetting a trespasser, uneasily evading her guardian's probing on whether it is right to teach her, or indeed to allow her at all, to read so deeply. Mr. Casaubon hedges: "Dorothea is learning to read the characters simply. . . . She had the very considerate thought of saving my eyes." But reading doesn't work by half measures. The more Dorothea reads in the subject of her husband's work, the more clearly she sees its, and his, smallness.

Mr. Casaubon is a paradigmatically bad reader, a man who approaches books entirely as a finite game in which personal power is at stake. Dorothea's sharp-eyed neighbor, Mrs. Cadwallader, delivers the novel's most memorable indictment of him:

> "He has got no red blood in his body," said Sir James.
> "No. Somebody put a drop under a magnifying-glass, and it was all semicolons and parentheses," said Mrs. Cadwallader.

One problem with an epigram this good is that it can obscure some important nuances. In this case it is true that one of Mr. Casaubon's many failings is a certain bloodlessness when it comes to his young and blooming wife—she spends her honeymoon seeing the sights of Europe alone while her husband buries himself in various archives. The implication is strong that her nights are similarly lonely. It would be easy to think of Casaubon, as his neighbors do, as a caricature of a man too given over to books to be useful in everyday life. Casaubon's impotence, in every sense of the word, however, is not caused by reading too much. It is an outward sign of his inability to read at all. Despite the years he has spent hiding in his books, Mr. Casaubon never gets lost in them. The surrender of self at the heart of reading is totally unknown to him.

Mr. Casaubon cannot give himself away. Instead, he clutches what little he has, grips and holds it, and in this way tries to keep it. He asserts himself in the face of his books and so shuts himself off from being fed by them. Ravenous, he consumes print while missing all the nutriment of reading. Maddened by his own hunger, he turns with malice on those who are full, demanding that they join him in starving. No one being fuller in this way than his young wife, Dorothea bears the whole burden of his need—she is the prime object of the vacuum inside him. Casaubon cruises easily beyond the wish that his wife have weak opinions to the demand that she have no self at all that is not a reflection of him. If his soul is small and cramped, yet echoingly empty, so must hers be. While he is alive, he can depend, however uneasily, on Dorothea's sense of duty to do the job of restricting her for him. Dorothea knows she is being treated unfairly, and protests silently at being required to "shut her best soul in prison, paying it only hidden visits, that she might be petty enough to please him." Nevertheless, she is kind, and in "look[ing] steadily at her husband's failure, still more at his possible consciousness of failure, she seemed to be looking along the one track where duty became tenderness."

As Casaubon nears death, however, he is not tender, or content with what a living wife may owe a living husband. Neither is he stupid. In digging a grave for Dorothea's soul, that she might climb into it when the time comes for him to lie in his own, he knows where to locate it: in the center of her life as a reader. Mr. Casaubon's life's work, the work he married Dorothea to help him with, his never-to-be-completed Key to All Mythologies, is a farrago of scholarly minutiae and resentments, an exhaustive map of Casaubon's own pettiness as a reader. Physically, it exists as a roomful of "abundant pen scratches and amplitude of paper." It is a mass of fragments, endless in number and as airless and meandering in their ideas as the "ante-rooms and winding passages which seemed to lead nowhither" of Casaubon's mind. This is the library to which Casaubon proposes Dorothea devote the rest of her reading life.

It is a living death and Dorothea knows it. So does Casaubon. The stakes could not be clearer in their final conversation on the matter. Neither of them even has to say exactly what it is Casaubon is asking her to promise.

"Before I sleep, I have a request to make, Dorothea."

"What is it?" said Dorothea, with a dread in her mind.

"It is that you will let me know, deliberately, whether, in case of my death, you will carry out my wishes: whether you will avoid doing what I should deprecate, and apply yourself to do what I should desire."

Dorothea was not taken by surprise: many incidents had been leading her to the conjecture of some intention on her husband's part which might make a new yoke for her. She did not answer immediately.

"You refuse?" said Mr. Casaubon, with more edge in his tone.

"No, I do not yet refuse," said Dorothea, in a clear voice, the need of freedom asserting itself within her; "but it is too solemn—I think it is not right—to make a promise when I am ignorant what it will bind me to. Whatever affection prompted I would do without promising."

"But you would use your own judgment: I ask you to obey mine; you refuse."

In fact, Casaubon is wrong. The next day Dorothea steels herself to assent, when Eliot, taking pity on her, has Casaubon drop dead seconds before Dorothea goes to see him. (Readers impatient with this authorial coup de foudre can turn to *Daniel Deronda*, in which a hardened Eliot requires her heroine to live out the full consequences of her decisions.)

Casaubon, with the authority of his culture behind him, is asking Dorothea to live out the most stringent terms of a Miltonic marriage contract: "hee for God only, shee for God in him." Few people love stringency more than Dorothea, a young woman born yearning to sacrifice herself for a great cause. Even her final decision to accede to her husband's request arises not from her fear of what he will do to her if she refuses, but from what she fears her refusal might do to him: "she could not smite that stricken soul that entreated hers. If that were weakness, Dorothea was weak."

Casaubon's crime, sanctioned though it is by law and tradition, is to demand that Dorothea ignore the gods in herself. Books are the way those gods make themselves known to her. Books are the means by which all readers hear the gods' voices (contradictory, fleeting, capricious) in a register we ignore only at a great cost. Our path through books, toward or away from any one of them, is not for anyone else to dictate. It is not even for us to understand. "What happens at the crucial moment, that of the choice . . . is not totally arbitrary, but nor can it be reconstructed through a finite series of steps. . . . While not being casual, the choice remains impenetrable, above all for he who has performed it." The "best" reading in the world is nothing if it is not our own. As Casaubon rightly notes, the question is one of freedom: he wants to substitute his judgment for Dorothea's—he wants her to commune with his gods to the exclusion of her own. This is an illegitimate thing to ask of anyone; it entails a suicide of the soul. Even as she considers complying with the request, Dorothea knows the shame is her husband's for asking it.

What suffering does Dorothea not bring down on herself by trespassing on the masculine territory of literacy? It opens inside her an unfeminine ambition to contribute to the world with "intensity and greatness," while showing her clearly how few paths to fulfilling that ambition her life is likely to provide her. It teaches her just enough to seize on Mr. Casaubon as her best hope of becoming part of a great achievement in learning, and only afterward reveals the extent of his unworthiness. If eagles do not actually tear at her liver, Dorothea nevertheless pays for her transgression with bitter suffering in the prison her marriage becomes. Even when that marriage dissolves in Casaubon's death, Dorothea is left with the wreck of her belief in an easy convergence of the road her soul longs to walk, and the one her world has laid out before her. Her reading is the light by which she sees, better than do most of her neighbors and all of her family, how much greater are the possibilities of human action and thought than those dictated by the traditions of her class. It is also the light by which she comes to recognize how tightly those traditions fetter even the most ardent woman born into them.

Suffer though she does, however, Dorothea is not a martyr. She transgresses by reaching for knowledge of freedom denied to her, and she pays for the transgression by knowing all the more acutely the boundaries of her confinement. Nevertheless, she also advances, even if only a step, toward widening those boundaries. Dorothea's capacity to surrender herself, a capacity excited, nourished, and focused by her reading, is not only a liability. As she matures, it shows itself to be the source not just of her worst mistake (marrying Casaubon, consigning her strength to his hopeless work) but also of her greatest achievements. She looks at Lydgate and sees vulnerability and disappointment where others see only pride; she looks at Rosamond and sees a child in need of guidance where others see only vanity; she looks at herself and sees a woman, still young, with little need of the social appurtenances her fellow townspeople think it is practically indecent to relinquish. Her fall into self-knowledge is steep and bruising, but it is also, like many falls before it, fortunate in its effects on the woman she becomes when she once again stands up. Casaubon's descent into tyranny is a cautionary tale about reading badly. Dorothea's suffering, and the expansion of her soul it facilitates, are potential effects of reading well.

IV

◆

Insight

Gertrude Stein wryly notes that "a great many things [in English literature] filled up everybody that had to be filled, of course it is only those that have an active need to be completely completed who have all this as a bother." With something like this idea in mind, the townspeople of Middlemarch are generally respectful of Dorothea's brains and learning, without taking them terribly seriously. It is as though she has been born with a slight impairment, enough to make them feel fond without causing them undue worry. No doubt they are right. If reading well requires a self strong and full enough to "get [it]self out of the way," the need to read at all feels as though it arises from an emptiness or an incompletion. All of us are born hungry, but some of us seem to be born without an enzyme necessary to our digestive system and find only in books the supplement we need to live. (Emily Dickinson: "I felt a palsy, here—the Verses just relieve—"). Without subjecting our experience to that process, without (to choose another metaphor) angling it through the prism of our reading, we can't quite know our own lives the way we need to. Once it begins, reading's action of reflection and refraction is so deep and seamless that its strangeness is easy to miss. It may be true that "our culture . . . is what makes us visible to ourselves." But through what process of recalibration do we see ourselves when we look into the distorted mirror of books? Why do some of us crave that distortion? What is it we see that we recognize as ourselves, often most powerfully when the reflection shows us a stranger?

Why should we need to be visible to ourselves at all? At best we may note that the need isn't unique to readers but defines human experience. Plato's *Symposium* provides a comic origin story for our searching after an image of ourselves. In it, Aristophanes proposes that we are descended from an ancient third gender, "globular" "men-wom[e]n" of such "strength and energy, and such . . . arrogance, that they actually tried . . . to scale the heights of heaven and set upon the gods." For their presumption, he says, Zeus split them in half, and ever since, we, for the sins of our parents,

> are all like pieces of the coins that children break in half for keepsakes—making two out of one, like the flatfish—and each of us is forever seeking the half that will tally with himself.

We try most often to find that other half in a human lover, but

> the fact is that [the soul longs] for a something else—a something to which [it cannot] put a name, and which [it] can only give an inkling of in cryptic sayings and prophetic riddles.

"Cryptic sayings and prophetic riddles" is Michael Joyce's 1935 translation of an idea Percy Shelley translated differently, in 1818: "something which there are no words to describe." Benjamin Jowett (1892) translates it as "something else which the soul . . . evidently desires and cannot tell, and of which she has only a dark and doubtful presentiment." Wallace Stevens, in 1951, is not explicitly quoting Plato, but might as well be, in positing that the poet gives the soul "that for which it was searching in itself and in the life around it and which it had not yet quite found." Plato was a writer, and so were his translators, so perhaps it is natural that their metaphors for the essential but ungraspable thing we lack involve words. Whether that missing thing exceeds words, or can be hinted at only indirectly, in coded and obscure words, or is something we know but cannot tell, no reader will be surprised to learn that the soul's work to recover it is done with words. It may be that the proliferation of words in writing, and the reader's drive to be surrounded by and immersed in books, is the equal and opposite reaction to the basic wordlessness into which we are born, that we use books as "stimulants, poultices, goads" in the face of a congenital and chronic condition of the soul. That condition, that sensing of something we lack, is itself part of what we need to see reflected in the curved mirror of literature, "which organizes everything / Around the polestar of [our] eyes." We read to fill the parts of us that are missing, but also to be affirmed in that sense of missing something in the first place. Books fill us, and they show us our yearning to be filled. A. R. Ammons's word for our feeling of incompletion is "longing." In his poem "For Harold Bloom" he creates a fable about that longing and the human creation that springs from it. It begins with a speaker on the top of a mountain who recognizes that he is fundamentally estranged from the world around him:

> I went to the summit and stood in the high nakedness:
> the wind tore about this
> way and that in confusion and its speech could not
> get through to me nor could I address it:
> still I said as if to the alien in myself
> I do not speak to the wind now:
> for having been brought this far by nature I have been

brought out of nature
and nothing here shows me the image of myself:
for the word *tree* I have been shown a tree
and for the word *rock* I have been shown a rock,
for stream, for cloud, for star
this place has provided firm implication and answering
but where here is the image for *longing*

The scientist in Ammons usually resists the idea that human beings are an exception to nature's workings. Rather than praise human vision as privileged, he more often celebrates its partialness. Because we are so involved in the systems we observe, he suggests, we should gratefully concede that "Overall is beyond" us and find serenity in the fact that outside the "narrow orders, limited tightness" of human understanding, "the looser, wider forces work." The writer in Ammons, however, who is also a reader of the Old Testament, feels and responds to a painful sense of division from the surrounding world, a division made acute by the always imperfect fit between what is most human about us—our language—and the world it describes. Our language is not the world's language. There is more in the world than we can name, but there is also more that our language names than we can find outside ourselves. If we are to find images that show us that excess, we will have to look to our own creation, as the speaker of Ammons's poem does:

I went back down and gathered mud
And with my hands made an image for *longing*:
I took the image to the summit: first
I set it here, on the top rock, but it completed
nothing: then I set it there among the tiny firs

but it would not fit:
so I returned to the city and built a house to set
the image in
and men came into my house and said
that is an image for *longing*
and nothing will ever be the same again

Placing his clay image here and there, Ammons's speaker learns twin truths: First, that nature, the world that is not-us, cannot complete us; nor can what we make complete it. Second, that the place for human creation is human habitations. Its audience is entirely human. Having faced an image for our own longing, which is to say, our own incompletion and exile, we leave with no promise of fulfillment or peace. All we know for sure is that we have encountered something that reflects us as we are.

It is a strange predicament we are in as readers. The soul longs for "something else," expressing that longing in "cryptic sayings and prophetic riddles," and in answer we surfeit her on more sayings, more riddles, endless tellings of what cannot, quite, be told. Perhaps it couldn't be otherwise, given that "it's a queer thing is a man's soul." It is "a dark forest" from which "gods, strange gods, come forth . . . into the clearing of [one's] known self, and then go back." We don't know what those gods want with us. There is little we can do to tempt or sway them. Instead, we try for "the courage to let them come and go," and we allow as many paths for their traffic as we can. We try not to block those paths with plans and intention and demands for immediate response. Meanwhile, we light our clearing—just enough to read by—because reading is a means of opening pathways beyond our control. And who knows? Perhaps gods are like moths and can be drawn from the dark.

There is a paradox at the heart of reading. The more absorbing we find it—the keener and less replicable elsewhere its joys are for us—the deeper becomes our sense that we read to get somewhere new, a place where books themselves might be unnecessary. A character in Joy Williams's *The Quick and the Dead* is visited by the unsentimental ghost of his ex-wife, who "point[s] to his books, his ties, even his travel alarm from Tiffany's, one of his favorite things," and says, "All this is unnecessary." Apparently, when seen through the eyes of the dead, books are bedside-table litter, tokens of our attachment to illusory notions of time, space, and the self no less than ties, clocks, and a taste for Tiffany. Living, we feel otherwise about them. Lacking the dispassion of the dead, we are guided by our sense that books are not quite like ties or travel clocks. Instead they are roads, passageways, breadcrumb trails, conduits, and escape routes. Most of the time we live in "that other world, unsyllabled"; only through books can we leave it.

Describing that passage is difficult. Even for the most fluent readers language is a code, and it retains traces of the feel of a mystery. It is not only "queerer than we suppose, but queerer than we can suppose." It is somewhere where we are not at home, where we are spoken to through a screen, indirectly. Even in our most rapt encounters with it, language doesn't lose that feel of hiding, enclosing, shrouding—of presenting a path that is also a barrier. Another Williams character describes reading as she once saw it from the outside, from the perspective of the uninitiated:

I suspected there was a trick to reading, but I did not know the trick. Written words were something between me and a place I could not go. My mother went back and forth to that place all the time, but couldn't explain to me exactly what it was like there. I imagined it to be a different place.

Is reading a different place? Williams's now-adult speaker leaves the matter in doubt, telling us what she imagined as a child, but not what she found when she finally learned the trick. How, in any case, could we be sure? While we are reading, wherever we are, we are in abeyance, out of our minds, in no position to judge. Then, when we return from a book, something about the world to which we return is different, if only "just a little different." It may be that the different place to which books take us is actually that remade ordinariness to which we return, the texture of our lives rewoven by our absence from it, our selves rewoven by what happened to us in that elsewhere. In this way reading is like dreaming, and subject to some of the same suspicions. Are dreams (are books) messages from parts of ourselves we can't otherwise bear to know? Is dreaming (is reading) a sacred experience or a kind of psychic housekeeping? Perhaps most crucially, are dreams (are books) an alternative to reality or an aspect of it? How do we know the difference between our real life and our dreaming (reading) life? What happens when the line gets blurred?

One name for what can happen is insight. If reading cannot promise to make us better, exactly, it nevertheless can shape the mind in ways propitious to broader and more patient encounters with the world and with ourselves. In those encounters we see more, and more clearly. Such moments of insightfulness involve a rapid, often unconscious diversion of our experience into un-expected channels. They feel effortless, as if imposed from without; suddenly, we know something we didn't know before. And yet they also feel internal, disclosing truths so secure we surely always knew them, truths that are ours. Insight arises less from pieces of new information than from moments of clarity about all that we are presently taking in—it is the point when a signal coalesces amid the noise. To be more precise about it the way it feels, it is as though the stream of our experience, flowing through us at all times, finds a previously unknown channel prepared for it, brought to life by the rush of waters through it. Searching for such channels is fruitless; they don't exist until the press of our consciousness finds them out. What we can do, however, is ready ourselves for their appearance, training ourselves to interfere as little as we can with the influx of our own experience.

Reception is insight's watchword, its sacred attitude, its ceaseless prayer position. Though it may involve waiting, and look like stillness, receptivity is an active state. It requires stamina to defer our impulses toward control and reaction. An attitude of reception involves above all a rootedness in self strong enough to tolerate the giving up of self. Becoming receptive, and staying that way, is the pathway to insight. Reading, pursued over a lifetime, is deep practice in reception. Alert, relaxed, keen, and unguarded, the reading self easily occupies an otherwise elusive and fleeting state of awareness in which no answer need be final, no one moment need be decisive. In that fluid medium insight is free to gather and effloresce. Several of Elizabeth Bishop's late poems depict experiences of insight, in which the poet arrives at an understanding achieved without effort, a power found without strain. Her easy synthesis, in "The End of March," of snarled string and large dog-prints into a fable about a deadly playful "lion sun," is one example. The apparition of the "grand, otherworldly" moose, following "a gentle, auditory / slow hallucination," in "The Moose," is another. She speculates about such moments in a letter:

> There is no "split" [between the role of consciousness and subconsciousness in art]. Dreams, works of art (some) glimpses of the always-more-successful surrealism of everyday life, unexpected moments of empathy (is it?), catch a peripheral vision of whatever it is one can never really see full-face but that seems enormously important. I can't believe we are wholly irrational— and I do admire Darwin! But reading Darwin, one admires the beautiful solid case being built up out of his endless heroic *observations*, almost unconscious or automatic—and then comes a sudden relaxation, a forgetful phrase, and one *feels* that strangeness of his undertaking, sees the lonely young man, his eyes fixed on facts and minute details, sinking or sliding giddily off into the unknown. What one seems to want in art, in experiencing it, is the same thing that is necessary for its creation, a self-forgetful, perfectly useless concentration.

Bishop, whose own poems are full of "endless, heroic observations" (she would have objected to the second adjective), is talking about herself as much as Darwin in this passage. In a poem called "Poem" she describes exactly such an experience of "sliding giddily" from a self-forgetful absorption in a work of art into a new understanding of one's own life. The poem's speaker is looking at a painting by a distant family member, allowing her attention to roam between the details of the paint and her speculations about the world it brings to life:

It must be Nova Scotia; only there
does one see gabled wooden houses
painted that awful shade of brown.
The other houses, the bits that show, are white.
Elm trees, low hills, a thin church steeple
—that gray-blue wisp—or is it? In the foreground
a water meadow with some tiny cows,
two brushstrokes each, but confidently cows;
two minuscule white geese in the blue water,
back-to-back, feeding, and a slanting stick.
Up closer, a wild iris, white and yellow,
fresh-squiggled from the tube.
The air is fresh and cold; cold early spring
clear as gray glass; a half inch of blue sky
below the steel-gray storm clouds.
(They were the artist's specialty.)
A specklike bird is flying to the left.
Or is it a flyspeck looking like a bird?

The speaker's attention is alert and wide-ranging. She is responsive to the painter's representational intentions ("The air is fresh and cold"), at the same time that she observes his technique, as in the iris "fresh-squiggled from the tube." She makes judgments ("that awful shade of brown," "confidently cows") and she entertains doubts ("a thin church steeple / —that gray-blue wisp—or is it?" "Or is it a flyspeck looking like a bird?"). There is no point to her looking, no goal to get in the way of the play between her eye, mind, and memory. She is able to look this way in part because the circumstances that brought the painting before her make no special claim on her time and focus. Earlier in the poem she describes the painting as "useless and free," earning no money, passing between various family-member "owners / who looked at it sometimes, or didn't bother to." Free from the structures of commerce and acclaim, the painting allows for a reading (not for nothing is this poem-about-a-painting called "Poem") that is similarly unencumbered. Because there is no particular reason the poet became one of the people who did bother to look at it, there is also nothing to get in the way of her looking.

And because she can freely receive what is before her, she can also see clearly what is inside her and inside others. "Heavens," she exclaims in the next stanza, "I recognize the place, I know it!" She has been looking intently, it turns out, at a landscape she can also just remember from her own past. In perusing his painting she has merged with her unknown artist relative: "Our visions coincided—'visions' is / too serious a word—our looks." The surprise of that coincidence is recognizing the specific pasture the two relatives saw many years apart, but the joy of it comes from the poet's feeling, in their merging, the shared experience simply of having lived. That joy arises, curiously, only when she loses herself in the details of art, with little thought of her individual self as a touchpoint. In marks on canvas she finds a memory reflected back to her as her own, but a memory transformed into a more than personal experience. It was art that began that transformation, and art's recipient that completed it. The painting brings her somewhere old and new at once. As Bishop's poem does for its own reader.

Notably, it takes Bishop's speaker some time to recognize a place she has already been. Her recognition is the opposite of efficient, an approach to the painting that sets aside any hierarchy of desires, including the most basic one we usually bring to a picture: that we can tell what it depicts. She does eventually learn this, but only after a period of deferral. Insight is born of deferral—the longer we defer our need to do anything with what we receive, the longer we have to take in what surrounds us. The hardest part of any encounter with art is the capacity to look steadily at it without asking it to conform to our own feelings about it or desires of it; although, when we do manage to look in this way, it is also the easiest part.

◆

The opposite of insight is obstruction, and there are no obstacles quite as effective as our own expectations. Because insight happens only by itself, in its own time, the trick is not to strain toward it but to steadily, repeatedly, remove the barriers we ourselves place in its way. *Ut pictura poesis*—as in painting, so in poetry. Bishop's portrait of the roving eye applies equally to the reader, moving back and forth between and among the lettered page and what it evokes in us.

Our reward for reading freely is the feeling that we have, just slightly, left both book and world behind. Nietzsche neatly catches the contradictory essence of this feeling when he asks, "What good is a book that does not even carry us beyond all books?" If the question sounds abstract, the experience it describes is visceral and familiar. When we have in hand a book that speaks to us, our pleasure in it, our thrill and expansion, push us beyond our tolerance for it. There are times when our reading is so good it causes us to look up from the page—when our reading is so good it makes us stop reading. We stop because we get near, in those moments, to something essential and unbearable. Reading narrows to a channel "an innavigable sea" that "washes with silent waves between us and the things we aim at and converse with." What are those "things," what is that something else?

"Power," "Divinity," the "Eternal," says Emerson. The "third rail," an "unbroken draught of poison," cautions Elizabeth Bishop. "The Truth," affirms Emily Dickinson, though she quickly warns that it "must dazzle gradually / or every man be blind."

Reading is an approach, a slant vantage from which we "[peep] into the unseen," peering "in the direction of the light-source." The light we look toward is also the light we read by. The light itself being too bright for our "finite eyes," we take it in indirectly, reflected off the page. The words we follow there, dark marks on a field of light, steady us—they are the shadows the light creates, shelters within the protection of which we absorb what illumination we can take. That light "has its centre where?" We don't know—it is somewhere "off behind the dunes," where it is "much too cold" to go. The light's exact location and nature are two of the "many things [that] are unsettled which it is of the first importance to settle." Meanwhile, "pending their settlement, we will do as we do," reading by the original light's infinite derivatives. "The first light of evening," "one late wicker-shaded lamp," "the waxing crescent-moon above the provinces," "the light of an electric torch," "a tongue of fire" in "a brimming / Saucer of wax," "great goblets of magnolialight" all are lights to read by. As such they are "perfect! But—impossible." Perfect, that is, for getting us started toward where reading wants to take us, but impossible to stay in long enough to get there. Light changes—it flickers, it fades, it gets too bright for us to take. What we see is subject to the light by which we see it—how can we trust what we know only through that changing medium? Light is "radiance" that "pours its abundance without selection" and "in no / way winces." But if light is dazzlement and revelation, it is also "maya, illusion," "the translucent mistake / of the desert" a lost wanderer could die trying to reach.

Light allows us to read and reading leads us to the light. Light is truth and tricks. Reading comes to us by way of the eye, and folk wisdom often teaches us to mistrust what we see: All that glitters is not gold. Don't judge a book by its cover. Seeing may be believing, but you can't believe everything you read. The complexities of writing, in which "letters are sounds we see," are vexing because the difference between seeing and hearing is enormous—there is no easy equivalence between them. Thus, reading leaves us in a visual world rooted in our ears and mouths, a place here and now and elsewhere and then. Describing it quickly involves one in a "House That Jack Built"–like cascade of cause and effect:

Here are the words before me.

Here are the signs for the words before me.

Here are the signs made up of the sounds for the written words before me.

Here is my mind roving to and away, among and between, the signs for the sounds for the trick of the light that brings to my eyes that learned from my brain to feel and to know the quietly present and gaudy and plain and stark and lush and historically linked and resonant words before me.

Reading is an impossible and perfect human creation by which individuals who are part of an immense totality of readers come in solitude to be "changed, healed, charged" by words that we made to do what we can't, in a place that would not exist except for our profound need for its existence.

Returning again and again to that place requires receptivity, but it also requires *faith*, because it offers few outward signs of its value. One argument against reading, at least in its promiscuous

variety, is that it lulls us into complacency and inaction, remov-
ing us from the real world of suffering, doubt, and tangible consequence where duty compels us to stay. Or if not duty, then a
healthy egotism. Why "invest [one's] life / In cloud banks" when
"the race [is] run below, and the point [is] to win"? Whether the
news on the ground is love or war, business or pleasure, the person
drawn to reading is likely also to have in her ear a voice as insis-
tent as a rooster's at dawn that keeps "screaming / 'Get up! Stop
dreaming!'" Reading is a willed and immersive illusion, a species
of dreaming, and the most passionate advocates of dreams teach
that they are devious, coded, misleading, full of traps for the un-
wary conscious mind. Why spend more time than is necessary in
a looking-glass world? Why go among mad people?

The poets, compromised by their vested interest in the question, are often little help in defending this practice. At best they
argue that living among the mad is inevitable—"you can't help
that . . . we're all mad here"—and at worst they simply invert the
terms of the argument: "Much Madness is divinest Sense." Poems, in describing what they do, give with one hand and take
away with the other. They offer a bottle labeled "DRINK ME"
that, when sipped, will make one exactly the wrong size to enter
the secret garden they promise. Or they hold out "a broken drinking goblet" from which they then propose, without irony, that
we "drink and be whole again beyond confusion." They demand
"imaginary gardens with real toads in them." They awake in us
a longing for "counter-love, original response," and then make
"nothing happen."

An internal voice, amplified by external claims on our attention, may also nag at us that art is by its nature a copy, a counter-
feit, a derivative, an echo rather than an answer. Worst of all is art
made of words, placed (it is commonly thought) already at the

distance of language from "real" life, and liable to spawn endless wordy responses, commentaries, and interpretations—in short, a parallel world of words with no end. People entranced by such language are easy targets of satire, like Mr. Casaubon, lost "in bitter manuscript remarks on other men's notions about the solar deities, [having] become indifferent to the sunlight." There is no use contesting the fact that language works, in every sense, by likeness. We connect words to things only by force of habit, by rules of play that are "ratified by collective agreement" but otherwise arbitrary. The relationship of language to things has no "therefore" to it, no essential quality of "must be." Instead there is only "is." I say "turtle" when others say "tortuga" or "sköldpadda." The animal itself, meanwhile, swims indifferently along, answering to names none of us will ever know; "the consequences which flow from this principle are innumerable." Reading is a double translation, from our earliest association of particular sounds with a set of meanings, to our later (but still breathtakingly early) association of visual marks with those sounds. Once our fluency in those equivalences is set, of course, language is no longer arbitrary in any meaningful sense. Our knowledge of a language is a real thing. Once one knows how to read, short of extraordinary trauma, one will not be able to help doing it. Literacy is a one-way street, "a machine that moves only forward."

But there was a moment before we stepped onto that road, and the fact that we are engaging in a translation so fast and practiced that we no longer feel it doesn't mean we aren't doing it. Reading is sifting and searching and surfing atop a wave of similitudes that never breaks. Words are never what they represent. At the same time, we never stop delighting in the feeling of order and connection in which the pleasure of language lives. We feel more than delight. It is, essentially, a tenet of readerly faith that language's cascade of likenesses can be a path to a unified reality. One of literature's recurrent dreams is that words can be put together in such a way that they will weave a new reality, in which there is no essential separation between word and thing. Reading can feel like entering such a world. The faith that such a world is possible fuels imaginative literature. Wallace Stevens articulates this faith most clearly (and most ambiguously) at the end of his essay "The Noble Rider and the Sound of Words":

> There is, in fact, a world of poetry indistinguishable from the world in which we live, or, I ought to say, no doubt, from the world in which we shall come to live, since what makes the poet the potent figure that he is, or was, or ought to be, is that he creates the world to which we turn incessantly and without knowing it and that he gives to life the supreme fictions without which we are unable to conceive of it.

There is a notable difference between a world "in which we live" and one "in which we shall come to live," as there is between what a poet "is" or "was" or "ought to be." Stevens makes no apologies for his equivocations, however. His subject, he explains, is "that nobility which is our spiritual height and depth." He continues:

> While I know how difficult it is to express it, nevertheless I am bound to give a sense of it. Nothing could be more evasive and inaccessible. Nothing distorts itself and seeks disguise more quickly. . . . But there it is.

Stevens's "nobility," the realm of souls, in which the world we know is also the world we create with words, in which truth is made manifest by means of "supreme fictions," is the reader's home. It is "noble" in the sense that metals or gases are said to be noble, resisting corrosion and reaction, whole in itself. More important, however, Stevens means by "nobility" a kind of spaciousness of the soul, "a release, if only provisional, from the cave of the dimmed and cramped self," a roominess in which we find ourselves "porous, resonant, unimpeded, incandescent." No one poem, or poet, can lead all of us to such spaciousness, or allow any of us to stay there permanently. The practice of reading, however, creates opportunities to sense the possibility of such space. The "noble" world into which reading creates entrances offers no proofs of its existence; we know it by our "thoughts and feelings which, we are sure, are all the truth that we shall ever experience." We learn our way along the way; we "learn by going where [we] have to go."

Stevens treats these elusive matters with full nuance in his poem "The Idea of Order at Key West." Throughout the poem, a woman walks by the ocean, singing. Meanwhile, her audience, the "we" who narrate the poem, notes the profound difference between her song and the sound of the ocean: the latter "Made constant cry . . . / That was not ours . . . / Inhuman." Her listeners also observe that "The water never formed to mind or voice," remaining indifferent to the human singing going on beside it. The two sounds are immiscible:

> The song and water were not medleyed sound
> Even if what she sang was what she heard,
> Since what she sang was uttered word by word.

The separation of a human song, made "word by word," from the ocean's cry, is absolute, and since the listeners are also human their allegiance is clear:

112

The . . . sea
Was merely a place by which she walked to sing.
Whose spirit is this? we said, because we knew
It was the spirit that we sought.

That spirit is powerful, and the listeners exult in it:

Then we,
As we beheld her striding there alone,
Knew that there never was a world for her
Except the one she sang and, singing, made.

And in fact, her song does seem to change the sea itself, just a little, for her audience too. As the sun sets and her song ends, the listeners turn toward a harbor and find that other signs of human work are newly triumphant in their environment. As they look at the harbor, still under the spell of the recently ended song, they see with wonder that "the lights in the fishing boats" suddenly act differently from before. Under the influence of the song, the lights, humble, utilitarian tools for navigation, suddenly "[master] the night and [portion] out the sea . . . / Arranging, deepening, enchanting night."

"The Idea of Order at Key West" is a fable about the strength of our faith in language. It proposes that the right words, ordered in the right way, make a world, and not just for the one who utters them, but for those of us who listen as well. Nevertheless, a lament like an undertow runs through the poem. However exhilarating it is that a song makes (or shall come to make, or once made, or ought to make) a new world, it remains a sorrow, for the singer and for us, that song and water will never be "medleyed sound." Making and mastering also entail separation: the singer is privileged and also condemned to walk beside the sea rather than to merge with it. Beneath the power of her song is the wound of this separation, the wound from which she sings at all, which is the same wound from which we listen. In the poem's final stanza, the speaker, one of the "we" who listen and are changed by the order of the singer's words, calls her singing a "blessed rage for order." Why a "rage"? In part because, as Stevens says elsewhere,

> From this the poem springs: that we live in a place
> That is not our own and, much more, not ourselves
> And hard it is in spite of blazoned days.

Language addresses this primal state of disconnection by bridging gaps between people. In doing so, it also draws attention to those gaps, repeatedly marking and mourning the place "where I end and you begin." "Good as is discourse," writes Emerson,

> silence is better, and shames it. The length of the discourse indicates the distance of thought betwixt the speaker and the hearer. If they were at a perfect understanding in any part, no words would be necessary thereon. If at one in all parts, no words would be suffered.

But it is not only other people from whom we are separated—the world around us also speaks a language not ours, with which ours will not be "medleyed." As A. R. Ammons has it, we find ourselves "Surrendered sel[ves] among / unwelcoming forms: stranger[s]," able only to "look and reflect" as "the air's glass / jail seals each thing in its entity."

◆

Nevertheless, it is given to us to make a home in a world not of us or for us. Our imaginative engagement with metaphor, an engagement that simply is what we talk about when we talk about reading, is one of the subtlest tools we have for doing so. *Metaphor* comes from the Greek for "transference." A metaphor "shift[s] a word or phrase . . . from its normal uses to a context where it evokes new meanings." We, as readers, are shifted along with the language, lifted from the tracks of our own thought into other ways of knowing. We are moved by metaphors, carried away, transported by them. In its simplest form, metaphor sets side by side two things that are different and proposes to the mind that they are alike. Metaphor does not change things, it asks us to consider them in the light they shine on one another. Everything looks different depending on the light in which we see it. The right metaphor educates and delights our sense of seeing. Pictured from above, a mountaintop glacier is "an octopus of ice." Summer hail is "the biggest size of artificial pearls." Our own bodies, imagined from within, are "house[s] whose rooms are pooled with blood." Each of these metaphors is true, in its way. Each expresses a truth of perception, in which a thing is known by virtue of the links we can forge between it and other known things, "everything only connected by 'and' and 'and.'"

Such links are endless by nature, so metaphor deals in a strain of truth in which finality is held just at bay, in which each new resemblance has a role to play in our understanding. By its nature metaphor releases us from "the perpendiculars, / straight lines, blocks, boxes, binds / of thought / into the hues, shadings, rises, flowing bends and blends of sight." Its most helpful use is in providing constant demonstrations, those "most effective of the modes of persuasion," to our binary-tending brains that "everything got four sides: his side, her side, an outside and an inside."

Writing of all kinds participates in metaphorical truth by inventing new likenesses. To the extent that language is an exchange of word for thing, it is essentially metaphoric. The simplest sentence engages us in the work of creating pathways across which to transfer ourselves from the world of the page to the world of our other experience, and then back. Good sentences, sentences that seem good to any given reader, open lasting routes, and interconnect ever more territory. It seems necessary for the soul's health that all territories be connected in the end, however distant from one another they seem at first.

In reading we participate in that work of connection by becoming a principle of action—words on the page show the map, and our reading bodies and brains walk it. All the better if we walk it half blind, out of our senses, without thought of a destination. D. H. Lawrence, an extraordinary reader, brings this wisdom to bear in reading Whitman:

> [The soul] is a wayfarer down the open road. . . .
> Only through the journey down the open road [does
> she come into her own].
> The journey itself, down the open road. Exposed to
> full contact. On two slow feet.
> In company with those that drift in the same measure
> along the same way.
> Towards no goal. Always the open road.

Books are one road for the soul, or they can be, so long as we walk "exposed to full contact," on "slow feet." The waywardness of our reading tells most here, in reading's function as soul-work. Reading works "internal difference / where the Meanings are," and those meanings are not ours to know beforehand, or to shape deliberately, except at the risk of limiting and deforming what is always on the cusp of blooming inside of us. Reading widely, freely, and constantly is a way of staying alive to the possibilities of chance, of affirming that "usefulness . . . has not been weaned from luck." More particularly, it is a way of living a faith in "luck" as a "neat pseudonym" for "the soul in her subtle sympathies accomplishing herself by the way."

It is no accident that Lawrence turns to poetry in articulating his soul sutra, slow and bare. A poem is among reading's slowest roads. "Everything ripens in the road," but ripeness takes time. It takes its own time, impervious to summary or skim, and offers little to show for it. The statement "I have read *The Recognitions!*" (or whatever the current day's massive monument to difficult pleasure is) is a piece of intellectual armor, a patch of clothing on one's naked self-regard. That is not the only thing it is, but it is often a happy side effect. Most poems are not like this. What is it to have read a poem well? To have caught an allusion, admired a formal twist, heard a music in the silent tumble of letters on the page? How long does it take to read a poem, anyway? Such reading does not proceed in continuous, countable units of hours and days. It is a minute, minutes, here and there, intense and distracted, questing, between trips to the dictionary, and it consists in endless, endless repetition. There is a great deal less reading than rereading where poems are concerned. A poem read once is the first note of a symphony, a toe dipped in the water, the first mouthful after a fast—necessary experiences all, with joys of their own, but still preludes. A poem comes into being by means of our repeated encounters with it, and each of these encounters must stay slow. It is hard to stay slow enough to keep pace with a poem.

The reward for moving without hurry is awareness. Where we are aware, possibility opens. A poem is a wide field on which possibility plays. It is a space in which, the longer we stay, the more expansive and intricate are the encounters we witness, between language and images and memory and emotion. "Interactions are everything" where a deepened capacity for response is at stake. When a poem "resist[s] the intelligence / Almost successfully," when a poem "tell[s] all the truth / but tell[s] it slant," when we are given a respite from the imperative to "MAKE SENSE OF IT," we are given a chance to allow sense to proliferate.

Which is not to say that the proliferation of sense is always easy. Unchecked multiplication can be beautiful in the context of flowers, queasy-making in the case of insects, and deadly in the cells of our own bodies. The persistence of a bell's resonance may be a pleasure to hear but would be intolerable if it didn't end. In the hands of a poet, language has no compunction for our limits. It will resonate as long and as complexly as we can stand, and every aspect of it is available for use. A poem has little respect for fair play when it comes to language—any resemblance, echo, implication, or linkage, however contingent, personal, fleeting, or outrageous, may be exploited. Reading poetry is falling "through a loophole of law and propriety and safety." There is a radical acceptance of equivalence in poetic language, a willingness to see, say, and celebrate the fact that things are like other things, which are like other things in turn. Immersion in equivalences comes at a cost, however, to the human desire that certain things be totally unlike and distinguishable from other things. For example, we would prefer that innocence not look like guilt. We would prefer that violence, savagery, and waste be wholly, and obviously, distinct from creation, art, and fulfillment. This not the way things work very often in life, or in poetry.

If reading exercises our capacities for reception and faith, then, it does so under conditions that require *fearlessness*. Lawrence's vision of the soul's slow progress, "exposed to full contact," makes no provision for squeamishness. In order to work in the soul's own manner, we are required to fall in with companions who "drift in the same measure along the same way." There is no guarantee that we will like the way those companions look, or what their similarity to us, their "drift[ing] in the same measure," will show us about ourselves. Reading asks us to stay open to what we encounter, and to keep faith that the likenesses we find are also paths to truth. Because of this, the ground of our receptivity and faith is courage in following metaphorical truth down any path it leads us. Poetry's ruthless harnessing of likeness, its root reliance on metaphor as a revealed form of meaning among the arbitrary workings of language, makes it a powerful tool for joining what has been sundered. Separation, isolation, are the wounds; poetry is a cure, never more so than in its capacity to join what would otherwise frighten, baffle, and disgust us in what we most love. The soul finds its companions without regard to pairings we would predict or necessarily accept. The soul puts everything together with everything else and sees what happens. As do fearless poets.

Few poets are more fearless in this way than Thylias Moss, a writer committed to registering without judgment or hesitation what the world presents her. In Moss's work there is no useful distinction between accidental and meaningful convergences. For her, every similarity is a link in the working of truth, especially when the links form between ideas, places, people, words, and things that otherwise present themselves as opposites and contradictions. Her poems are merciless exercises of her gift that teach bravery, both aesthetic and moral, to the reader who joins her in them. They are bright emblems of the fearlessness reading cultivates. Her poem "The Subculture of the Wrongfully Accused" is a case in point. The poem is about a miscarriage of justice, a real-life case in which a woman, Jennifer Thompson, misidentified a man, Ronald Cotton, in a lineup as her rapist. Later, when DNA evidence exonerated Cotton and identified the actual rapist as Bobby Poole, Thompson asked Cotton's forgiveness and the two together became advocates for DNA testing in rape cases. Moss's interest in the story is in the mystery and consequences of resemblance, the force on which poetry depends. She finds resemblances everywhere: Cotton watches, from a window in solitary confinement, a cardinal eating snails, which are like his own coiled hair; the witnesses at his trial, like insects visiting a cotton flower, "taint . . . / what is put out, taken in; mix // it up so that interrelatedness spreads"; his own calm demeanor is taken for lack of emotion, his innocence reflected in a "Poole" that made it look like "something else." Moss sees the intertwinement of life and language, including all manner of puns and homophones, as grist for the soul trying to understand its place in the world. In her poems "there is no use hesitating before a coincidence," because in the world where the soul lives nothing that happens is mere happenstance, there is no ground that is not also figure, and no basis on which the artist could easily sort the resemblances that matter from those that don't. "Many lives changed," Moss writes: "because the fact of similarity is compelling, convincing." That similarity resulted in protracted injustice for Ronald Cotton, but Moss nevertheless insists on its final value:

if connections could not be made, there'd be no
    havens, no fugitive
status lost to fusion, no links to God

Moss calls Thompson's certainty in identifying Cotton as her attacker, and her later work to publicize his innocence, "dazzling," "another side" of the ongoing conundrum of the curious mis-fit between "life and the memory of it." Thompson and Cotton, white and Black, female and male, accuser and accused, separately wronged, "team up" in Moss's poem to form an image of metaphor itself:

Metaphor is a form of forgiveness; a short rope of it
    knots-up
those that can't come together any other way into
    being defined
by the other. Strange

and estranged pairings give rise to mutable truth
that can yield to both dawn and twilight
demands that things be seen differently.

In "The Subculture of the Wrongfully Accused" the story of Thompson and Cotton exemplifies the way in which seeing a thing differently, which is a useful working definition of the action of metaphor, is the catalyst for a chain of forgivenesses: Jennifer Thompson need not always mean false accusation and unjust imprisonment for Ronald Cotton; Ronald Cotton can mean for Jennifer Thompson the transformation of victimhood into justice. The story's knotting together of innocence and guilt, injustice and justice, Black and white, man and woman, embodies our hope that no evil need be final, that a good tree can be grafted onto a bad root and flourish.

Forgiveness and hope, however, are not necessary outcomes of metaphor's work. In her poem "The Culture of Funnel Cake" Moss's descriptions of metaphor are harsher:

> [. . .] metaphor
> is king of advocating forced symmetry: ropes, chains
> full of burqua look-out opportunities:
>
> there is no isolation, no exile, no uniqueness
> it can't cure, finding not dreaded duplicates
>
> but equivalences, *almosts*, and *not quites*, *make dos*: in
>   the name of surrogacy
> the Tree of Evolution spikes and branches,
> veers: therefore such amazing twigs: those angels,
>   those demons,
> those despots and lovers among us.

In poetry, as Moss has it, the tree in question is not the Tree of Life or the Tree of Knowledge, but the Tree of Evolution. That tree branches as easily into demons as it does into angels, into despots as easily as lovers. Seen as a branching of this tree, the most salient feature of the story of Cotton and Jennifer is the element of chance that underlies it. Evolution is the process by which unpredictable mutation, random in itself, becomes a meaningful factor in a species' survival. Cotton's resemblance to the actual rapist, a resemblance grounded in a specific cultural context as well as a physical set of features, is one such mutation.

Jennifer's need for justice seized onto that resemblance as readily as her later need to make restitution repudiated it. If metaphor is a form of forgiveness, Moss means "forgiveness" in an impersonal sense: in metaphor things give up their claims to division and difference, coming together without regard for what formerly kept them apart. There is no guarantee that such comings together result in something beautiful or useful. Poetry's curative metaphor, the demand "that things be seen differently," is a hard discipline, requiring poet and reader alike to exercise a more than human energy in the service of a power that is exhilarating in its capacity to bring things together, and dangerous because it does not care what it brings together, while we, who must live with its consequences, do.

And because we are Plato's half-persons, torn apart and searching for what will make us whole again, we care very much. We are the things metaphor brings together. The "isolation, exile, uniqueness" in need of a cure are our own. Literature's lesson is that that cure will arrive provisionally, repeatedly, and in forms we could never expect beforehand. Since we cannot know what our complement looks like, we keep reading ourselves into the place where metaphor can do its work, "try[ing] each thing" alongside every other thing to see what wholes may arise. That this work is endless, bound to result in *almosts*, and *not-quites*, *make-dos*" is no reason to stop. It is simply life on a human scale. Final perfection, ultimate healings of division, is the stuff of myth: a state of grace we intuit and long for and aspire to, while persisting in our split and imperfect lives. In our present forms we could probably not survive the cure for our separateness if we found it. Nevertheless, we can read and stay open to strange arrivals, playful and transgressive "words . . . of ourselves and of our origins." We can, we have to, keep reading.

V

◆

Conclusions

1. Once upon a time . . .

Imagine a story, both myth and fairy tale, of wholeness ruined by a fall into separation. Once upon a time the word was breath. Stories lived and died with those who told them. To learn was to hear, to teach was to speak. Knowledge was felt in the mouth, like fruit, and in the delicate bones of the ear, like music. Wisdom was synonymous with the collective. Great learning meant the merging of the individual into the wide sea of voices gone before. The mind left traces only on other receptive minds, so words were both evanescent and tangibly powerful. Only living presence mattered in the transmission of knowledge. Only living presence formed a link strong enough to the past to tell people who and what they were in the present.

One day, amid this bliss, the envious eye and abetting hand began whispering to each other like serpents. Sometimes they spoke arrogantly: They had so much power of their own. Why should they be subordinate to voice in the matter of knowledge? Why not its equals? Sometimes they sounded conciliatory, reasonable: Surely they could at least do more to assist knowledge than they had so far been allowed? Their particular technologies were just waiting to be of service.

It would be hard to say which mood governed them at the moment when they finally acted:

> Once, self-determination
> made an axe of a stone
> and hacked things out with hairy paws. The
> consequence—our mis-set
> alphabet.

That alphabet's success exceeded anything its creators could have imagined, largely because imagination itself became intertwined with the letters it made. Writing took hold and transformed the nature of knowledge: "From then on, nondiscursive thought was to be pushed aside, or even underground." What was resonant became visual, so that "sounds leap[t] to the eye. . . . Letters [were] scrawls, turnabouts, astonishments, strokes, cuts, masks." Words, once "occurrences, events," "exist[ing] only when . . . going out of existence," became objects, manipulable like toys by restless minds, and adored like idols by the susceptible. It was forgotten that written marks were only ever intended to be crude arrows pointing back toward the truth of breath in body. Once it had been contemptible, shameful to write down sacred formulas; now only what was written down had authority. Authority, originality, creation itself, were believed to be within human power. Making, poesis, became synonymous with the individual, rather than with a community attentive to its history and its gods. Difference, disruption, distinction, novelty, and reinvention became ascendant gods. A new dogma arose, a direct refutation of what had gone before: "The sound of a word is not in itself important, but the phonetic contrasts which allow us to distinguish that word from any other." Things have gone so far that now, in our present Iron Age, it can be said without a shred of self-consciousness that "the object in writing poetry is to make all poems sound as different as possible from each other."

2. (Cherchez la femme.)

(Naturally, women were a special exacerbation of every ill attendant on this fall. Their well-known failings—vanity, mental chaos, lax moral sense—drew them especially powerfully to the glittering lure of letters, despite all that could be done to dissuade them. It was bad enough that writing had displaced speech, but it was intolerable that writing made no distinctions among those who read it and, inevitably, among those who performed it. Sensible precautions were taken, as they still are. Women were prohibited from learning letters at all. Where that proved impossible, or simply inconvenient, they were prohibited from learning the sacred languages, and at the very least prohibited from studying the sacred texts. That strategy, however, was only partially successful and, one could argue, had consequences worse than the problem it set out to solve. Women began reading and writing in demotic languages, and their unique influence over children meant that a generation of would-be enforcers of the division between sacred and profane came themselves to waver in their commitment to the sacred. Men began writing in their mother tongues.

For a long time many of our best minds put their trust in belittling those subjects traditionally associated with women: the home, children, relationships between ordinary men and women. Even that tactic, however, marvelously subtle and durable as it has proved to be, has lately shown signs of weakening. Allowing the novel a place among intellectually respectable objects of study was a fatal error in strategy. It was simple hubris to think that admitting a form so dominated by female practitioners, so inseparable in its origins from the minutiae of domestic life, would not lead to the erosion of distinctions between male and female, high and low, true and untrue. It may be that we must finally destroy reading if we are serious about saving it from the wrong people.)

3. The vale of soul-making.

Happy and not, our fall into literacy was accomplished long ago. Now we live in its permanent, ever-emergent aftermath. The written word, irrespective of the delivery systems by which we receive and transmit it, is and has been for centuries the dominant technology in every aspect of our civic life. Under its dominion, ease in the codes of written language is, while not a sufficient means to health and prosperity, nevertheless an emphatically necessary one. The issue is urgent. According to the UNESCO Institute for Statistics, in 2016, the latest year for which data are available, the global literacy rate stood at 86 percent. Of the 750 million of the world's adults who lacked basic reading and writing skills, two-thirds were women. The regions of the world with the lowest literacy rates (the report cites northern and western Africa, South Asia, and sub-Saharan Africa) also had the greatest gender gaps in their populations' literacy and are among the world's poorest. In the United States, according to the 2003 National Assessment of Adult Literacy (NAAL), approximately thirty million adults possess "below basic" literary skills. This means they cannot perform "simple and everyday literacy activities" or "use printed and written information to function in society, to achieve [their] goals, and to develop [their] knowledge and potential." Among these thirty million people, Hispanic and Black adults are significantly overrepresented, as are those with multiple disabilities. According to a 2014 survey conducted by the Program for International Assessment of Adult Competencies (PIAAC), nearly one-third of the U.S. prison population scored below level 2 on the assessment's literacy scale. In other words, nearly one-third of people imprisoned in the United States are able at best to "make low-level inferences based on what they read and integrate two or more pieces of information," and another third may or may not be able to "read short pieces of text to find a single fact [or] enter personal information on a document." The costs of these levels of illiteracy are catastrophic: lack of employment, poorer health, and shorter life spans for individuals, measurable loss of gross domestic product for nations. It is no exaggeration to say that at this moment in human history a solid foundation in literacy is essential to "Life, Liberty and the pursuit of Happiness."

In the world we currently live in, then, literacy per se is a different matter from reading in its more specialized sense as a chosen path of inquiry. Literacy is a human right, an individual competence inextricable from social health. Access to it is a question of social justice, a nonnegotiable entitlement of citizenship. To say, as one of this book's initial propositions does, that not everyone has to be a reader is different from saying that not everyone should to be taught to read. Everyone has a fundamental right to learn to read. A society in which people are actively denied literacy, or a society that neglects literacy in wide segments of its population, has reason to be ashamed. If the ascendance of the written word may be imagined as a fall from the original paradise of oral culture, the labor with which we are tasked for that primal transgression is making the world of writing available to all comers. It is an enormous labor, requiring unflagging, communal commitment.

At the same time, it would be an error to jump from acknowledging the universal necessity of literacy to exalting literacy as the best means of soul-making. Reading is a distinctly human capacity, but so is looking at images, so is listening to music. If we are lucky, we learn to read as young children, but even so, reading usually enters our lives later than singing and drawing and dancing and building and, in short, the whole array of ways we may later continue to step away from ourselves and in doing so enrich our lives. Everyone has a soul to tend. No one has a final answer about the soul's care and feeding. Even the most devoted reader has ample evidence that this is so, and the broader-minded among us acknowledge that reading has no special claim to be better than other answers. Keats, for example, reflects on the infinity of ways in which human souls are made in a letter to his brother and sister-in-law. Written while he was reading about the conquest and settlement of America, and about seventeenth-century France, the letter describes the effect of that juxtaposition on his thinking about the relative destinies of men in "natural" and "civilised" life. Comparing men "as it were estranged from the mutual helps of Society and its mutual injuries" to those beset by "Baliffs, Debts and Poverties of civilised Life," he concludes that "Man," into whatever form of civilization he is born, is "destined to hardships and disquietude of some kind or other." Nevertheless, Keats is impatient with those who call the world a "vale of tears," insisting instead, "Call the world if you Please 'The vale of Soul-making.'" While he allows that "there may be intelligences or sparks of the divinity in millions," he asserts that "they are

not Souls till they acquire identities, till each is personally itself."
"How then," he asks,

> are Souls to be made? How then are these sparks which are God
> to have identity given them—so as ever to possess a bliss pecu-
> liar to each one's individual existence? How, but by the medium
> of a world like this?

By "a world like this" he means "a Place where the heart must
feel and suffer in a thousand diverse ways." The result of our diversity in feeling and suffering, he says, is the variety of the world's
souls, "as Various as the lives of Men are." This variety includes,
in Keats's day as now, and always, the countless people, past and
present, who don't choose to spend their time reading.

4. "The *Child able to read*."

Even Keats, however, cannot stay very long away from literate
metaphors when the shaping of human souls is under discussion.
Without doubting his sincerity in contemplating the infinite ways
in which people make their souls, the confirmed reader is also
likely to enjoy the way his particular art comes back to him in the
final phase of his speculation. In attempting to put his idea of the
"vale of soul-making" "in the most homely form possible," Keats
metaphorically returns reading to pride of place among the many
human tools for the soul's cultivation. He writes:

> I will call the *world* a School instituted for the purpose of teach-
> ing little children to read—I will call the *human heart* the *horn
> Book* [a primer used to teach children the alphabet] used in that

School—and I will call the *Child able to read, the Soul* made from that *School* and its *horn book*.

One pleasure of watching children learn to read is seeing their delight when they first realize how much of their environment is in fact legible. Billboards, signs, labels, objects in their own houses—all of them turn out to be covered with words. Suddenly, the world is a landscape that communicates in a new way, that has always been communicating, just waiting for a reader to receive it. That experience gets forgotten as we age, but it leaves as its mark our longing that such revelations might persist, that the world might continue to surprise us by writing to us in a language we can read. What reader can blame Keats for his final metaphor, in which the soul simply *is* the child reading? That is what reading can feel like—like the soul doing its mysterious, unmistakable work. Reading brings us close to an understanding of things, to a hidden harmony, a design, a universal language just beyond the tip of our tongue.

If only everything were a book! It feels as though everything might be, if we could just read a little bit better. That dream haunts the reading mind. It is a wish that shows up when that kind of mind wanders to its longing for connection. "What was it that nature would say?" wonders Emerson, in such a mood; "was there no meaning in the live repose of the valley behind the mill, and which Homer or Shakespeare could not re-form for me in words?" Emerson, modestly, assumes he needs the intervention of the greatest writers in order to become a reader of the world around him. Whitman, in a more confident vein, proposes that he is one of those writers, and that it is his appointed job to read the world directly: "To me the converging objects of the universe perpetually flow, / All are written to me, and I must get what the writing means." Emily Dickinson feels the same imperative, describing moments that come to her in which she can see

> The eager look—on Landscapes—
> As if they just repressed
> Some Secret—that [is] pushing
> Like Chariots—in the Vest—

Readers today are no less half in love with the idea that the world is a book awaiting its reader. Susanna Clarke, imagining the resurgence of magic in a fictionalized England of the nineteenth century, recurs to Whitman's image in describing magic's effect on a receptive character:

> The birds were like black letters against the grey of the sky. He thought that in a moment he would understand what the writing meant. . . . The brown fields were partly flooded; they were strung with chains of chill, grey pools. The pattern of the pools had meaning. The pools had been written on the fields by the rain.

Magic, as Clarke imagines it, is simply the dissolving of the code encrypting the world's writing from human understanding. David Foster Wallace's *The Pale King* begins with a fragment set in the American Midwest, but otherwise directly heir to Emerson and Dickinson's longing, and akin to Clarke's vision of what we might do with the world if we were no longer estranged from it:

> The pasture's crows standing at angles, turning up patties to get at the worms underneath, the shapes of worms incised in the overturned dung and baked by the sun all day until hardened,

there to stay, tiny vacant lines in rows and inset curls that do not close because head never quite touches tail. Read these.

Taken together, these writers suggest that if one readerly worry is that there will never be enough time to read all the books, another, more serious one, is that we won't even recognize the important books when we see them.

5. "Where is a book before you read it?"

The question suggests itself in the work of Lynda Barry, who asks, "Where is a story before it becomes words?" and "Where is a story after it becomes words?" Each question is more koan than query. Books as objects are (for those who are lucky) scattered everywhere nearby. Books as experiences of reading, however, "books" in the sense of a particular meeting of minds, are where? Is the you that you will become while reading already in existence when someone has written what will precipitate that you? Or does the book conjure it from nothing? An apt companion question might be "Where are you before you have read a book?" Most readers have an experience that approaches both questions negatively, when we read a book that does not change or transport us. Not all books are for everyone. If a book is not for us, if it does not mean something to us, if it does not take us out of ourselves while reading it, it does not in any important sense exist for us. Such a book is nowhere before, during, or after our reading of it. "Reading" such a book is a contradiction in terms. If feelings can be trusted, we can really only read what is ours to begin with.

This truth makes teaching literature a tricky business. The point of reading is to do work (to do play) that is so intimate, so foundational to the soul's development, that it becomes difficult to describe, let alone design a curriculum around. We can make guesses about books that will be important to students, we can lead them to the books that have mattered to others, and we can help them develop habits of concentration, investigation, and reflection that are necessary to reading at any stage of life, but so much can go wrong in the process. So much is practically guaranteed to go wrong when education (a system in which engagement is mandatory) meets reading (a practice that is voluntary, or it is nothing). There is a real danger that books can be killed for readers simply by being introduced too early, in the wrong context, by the wrong teacher. How many high school students have been dissuaded from reading George Eliot ever again by first having been required to read *Silas Marner*? How many readers are lost every day because they learn that reading means performing mastery over a test, rather than losing oneself altogether?

But then, how many readers found in school the only refuge for reading they had? Or met there, for the first time, an adult as drawn to books as they were? Moreover, the adolescent who was once assigned *Macbeth* will become the adult who thereafter knows about it, irrespective of what she got out of it at the time, and it is easier to find things we need when we already know they exist. Formal education rarely offers perfect introductions to its subjects, but introductions don't need to be perfect to nonetheless create useful road maps. Books that don't exist for us at twenty may transform us at forty, and vice versa.

In any case, readers who have persisted in reading long after anyone was looking over their shoulder while they did it have of necessity absorbed, grown from, and overcome the myriad encounters with books from which we all start. What matters is staying attuned to an ordinary, unflashy, mutely persistent miracle: that all the books to be read, and all the selves to be because we have read them, are still there, still waiting, still undiminished in their power. Even if we never learned a new word from now on there would remain an unlimited number of ways to order the ones we know into books that will change us when we encounter them. It is an astonishing joy.

6. A modest proposal.

Meanwhile, if we need an avatar of that joy, we might bear in mind the twelve-year-old girl. Her reading habits reward study and emulation. How does she read? She reads a lot, for one thing, often when other people would prefer she didn't. At the dinner table is a good time, or at lunchtime at school, surrounded by friends. Bedtime is a given, but the beach works fine too, as do family gatherings of all kinds. Reading is an invaluable resource for the dead time classrooms are likely to provide. Rereading is so instinctively pleasurable that she is several years away from notic- ing that adults rarely seem to do it. She is in fact years away from understanding that not everyone hoards books or feels relieved to be left alone with them. She is a literary omnivore, reading, since reading is a matter of life or death, self or no self, the way wild animals eat. The best books are the ones right in front of her— she may have preferences, but she gorges on what she finds. She is just shy of knowing that some books are better than others, in the sense that those books will make her look and feel smart for reading them, or at least owning them, or in a pinch just knowing which ones they are. She is innocent. She is an amateur in a world run by professionals.

It is in poor taste, culturally speaking, to operate like an adolescent girl. Who has less power than she does? Whose voice is "shriller," whose obsessions are more easily dismissed and mocked, who will more predictably be easier to ignore as she enters adulthood? Adolescence is no fun for boys either, but, at least in the realm of literature, different attitudes await them on the other side. Their obsessions—say, the baby-boomer holy trinity of masturbation, baseball, and comic books—have for several generations now been the stuff of prizewinning literary fiction. When the time comes for men to put away childish things, they do not have to apologize for them. On the contrary, they can count on broad empathy and an audience ready to admire how skillfully the absorptions of male youth get transmuted into the mature work of male artists.

"The Child is the father of the Man" in a way our twelve-year-old is not yet, not quite, at least in our literary imagination, the mother of the woman. We are only beginning to know, collectively, what binds adolescent girls. But an immersion in books is often one thing that does. In describing what being "literary" really is, C. S. Lewis imagines a family that plumes itself on its up-to-date taste in books, led by adults who "drop the Georgians and begin to admire Mr. Eliot . . . at exactly the right moment." "Meanwhile," he notes approvingly,

> The only real literary experience in such a family may be occurring in a back bedroom where a small boy is reading *Treasure Island* under the bed-clothes by the light of an electric torch.

It is happening in his sister's bedroom, too, where she is reading Frances Hodgson Burnett, Louisa May Alcott, L. M. Montgomery, Susan Cooper, E. L. Konigsburg, Pearl Buck, Margaret

Mitchell, Louise Fitzhugh, Helen Van Slyke, Madeleine L'Engle, Ursula Le Guin, Judy Blume, Ellen Raskin, Paula Danziger, and Virginia Hamilton. That girl, lost in her reading, is primed, like children of any gender in the industrialized world, to have her enthusiasms, interests, and tastes packaged and sold back to her. Because she is female, she is also primed to be taught that her enthusiasms are vapid, her interests shallow, her taste in need of revamping. Boyishness in general will be an attractive quality in a man, suggesting enthusiasm, humor, vitality, openness, and freedom. Girlishness (unless, sometimes, applied to her looks) will have less to recommend it, referring mainly to the parts of a woman's character and habits that interfere with her authority. We have a useful word for the male person who can move easily between ages and roles and interests and aspirations: we call him a guy. When we are comfortable with a similar flexibility in his female counterpart, we will find a word for her too. Nevertheless, in the meantime, if we are lucky, and resilient, and vigilant about respecting our instinct for what feeds us best, grown men and women can practice reading like girls. It goes like this: pick up a book and forget who you are.

Notes

I. PROPOSITIONS

3 "right alongside": Spiotta, 91.

3 "commodity inclusive": Moore, "Old Tiger," *New Collected Poems*, 291.

3 "dream with our eyes open": Chabon, 98.

3 "separate and alone": DeLillo, *Underworld*, 89.

3 "driving to the interior": Bishop, "Arrival at Santos," *Poems*, 88.

3 "changed, healed, charged": Wright, *Cooling Time*, 55.

3 "the repository": Rose, 40.

3 "single, immobile and solitary act": Calasso, *Literature and the Gods*, 22.

3 "all the powers": Ibid.

3 "a betrayal": Birkerts, 37.

3 "held precariously": O'Hara, "Poem," *Lunch Poems*, 21.

3 "It seems, in the last analysis": Stevens, "The Noble Rider and the Sound of Words," *Collected Poetry and Prose*, 665.

4 "living option": James, "The Will to Believe," *Writings*, 458.

4 "perfectly useless": Bishop, *Poems, Prose, and Letters*, 860.

5 "potential space"; "an area that cannot": Winnicott, 69.

5 "The actual world"; "The reader is there": Wright, *Cooling Time*, 91.

5 "we have to stand on tiptoe": Thoreau, 104.

5 "only words that enlarge": Hirshfield, "Thoreau's Hound: Poetry and the Hidden," *Ten Windows*, 104.

6 "Why not be alone": Moore, "Marriage," *New Collected Poems*, 63.

6 "a spontaneous gathering": Carse, *The Religious Case*, 84.

6 "dependent on rulers": Ibid.

7 "*Homo sapiens*": Ong, 2.

7 "Of all the many": Ibid., 7.

8 "Thinking of oral tradition": Ibid., 12.

8 "If men learn [writing]": Hamilton, *Phaedrus*, *The Collected Dialogues of Plato*, 520.

9 "Written words . . . seem": Ibid., 521.

10 "is both a map": Wallace, *Everything and More*, 14.

10 "only just now": Nietzsche, *Human*, *I*, 21.

10 "In short, our gentleman": Cervantes, 21.

10 "[My father] buys me": Dickinson, *Letters*, 404.

11 "waiting with all": Cervantes, 46.

11 "no enchanter": Ibid., 45.

12 "transitional objects": Winnicott, 17.

12 "down, down in the terrestrial": Dickinson, *Letters*, 181.

12 "the choice is never wide": Bishop, "Questions of Travel," *Poems*, 92.

13 "Admittedly [we] err": Merrill, *The Book of Ephraim*, *The Changing Light at Sandover*, 3.

13 "only [have] at heart": Frost, "Directive," *Collected Poems, Prose & Plays*, 341.

13 "USE USE USE": Adapted from Merrill, *The Book of Ephraim*, *The Changing Light at Sandover*, 15.

13 "We shall have to resign": Calasso, *Literature and the Gods*, 176.

13 "sets the hairs": Ibid.

13 "new shiver": Ibid.

14 "If I read a book": Dickinson, *Letters*, 473–74.

14 "the genuine"; "eyes that can dilate": Moore, "Poetry," *New Collected Poems*, 27.

14 "force and beauty": James, *Letters*, 536.

14 "in states of absorption": Phillips, 40.

14 "Even and especially": Wright, *Cooling Time*, 10.

15 "There are those": Manguel, 19–20. Manguel is quoting Ezequiel Martínez Estrada.

15 "stop somewhere": Whitman, "Song of Myself," *The Complete Poems*, 124.

15 "perfect contempt": Moore, "Poetry," *New Collected Poems*, 27.

16 "Since . . . the knowledge": Milton, *Areopagitica*, *Complete Poems and Major Prose*, 729.

16 "I cannot praise": Ibid., 728.

17 "she didn't read books": Hurston, 76.

17 "we must never assume": Lewis, 48.

18 "The discovery that you are": Carse, *Finite and Infinite Games*, 69.

18 "valentines and messages of state": Moore, "Pigeons," *New Collected Poems*, 121.

18 "A light to read by": Bishop, "The End of March," *Poems*, 200.

18 "Zeus . . . would not entrust": Hesiod, *Theodicy, Works of Hesiod*, 73.

19 "See your Declaration": Walker, 85.

20 "Legislators in Georgia": McHenry, 31.

20 "South Carolina—Act of 1740": Goodell, 319–20.

21 "I soon perceived": Shelley, *Frankenstein*, 81.

21 "Mistress, in teaching me": Douglass, *Narrative of the Life of Frederick Douglass, Autobiographies*, 40.

22 "after considerable thinking": Brown, 25.

22 "[Zeus] bound": Hesiod, 71.

23 "Sorrow only increased": Shelley, *Frankenstein*, 83.

23 "As I read and contemplated": Douglass, *Narrative of the Life of Frederick Douglass, Autobiographies*, 42.

23 "The first demand": Lewis, 19.

24 "We sit down": Lewis, 19.

24 "get yourself out of the way": Ibid.

24 "One must be an inventor": Emerson, "The American Scholar," *Essays & Poems*, 59.

24 "tenacious, acquisitive, tireless": Whitman, "Song of Myself," *The Complete Poems*, 70.

25 "What should be"; "A good housewife": Thoreau, 36.

25 "take an axe and pail": Ibid., 282.

25 "grow double": Wordsworth, "The Tables Turned," *Selected Poems and Prefaces*, 107.

26 "The student may read Homer": Thoreau, 100.

27 "We have the conscience": Nietzsche, *Human, II*, 223.

27 "Reading was what I used to do": Schwartz, 12.

27 "the pleasantry of a cat": Smart, "Jubilate Agno," *Selected Poems*, 101.

28 "A book must be the axe": Kafka, 16.

II. PLAY

31 "It offers many": Costikyan.

31 "it / is permissible": Moore, "Peter," *New Collected Poems*, 46.

31 "The game is not intrinsic": Costikyan.

32 "make one little room": Donne, "The Good Morrow," *The Complete English Poems*, 60.

33 "contains within itself": Cervantes, xxii. From Harold Bloom's introduction.

33 "As for your grace's": Ibid., 472.

34 "spent his nights reading": Ibid., 21.

34 "There are at least two": Carse, *Finite and Infinite Games*, 3.

35 "Tell me, do you not see": Cervantes, 153.

35 "the opposite of play": Chai, "Primordial Subjects," *Standing Water*, 47.

35 "Pay me what you owe me": Cervantes, 121.

36 "parody . . . become a paragon": Nabokov, 112.

36 "vision of life": Carse, *Finite and Infinite Games*, subtitle.

36 "To be playful": Ibid., 15.

36 "it was an evil moment": Cervantes, 308.

37 "That Don Murray": Saunders, "My Chivalric Disaster," *Tenth of December*, 211.

38 "I attempted to Comfort": Ibid., 214.

38 "the passage of the mind": Calasso, *Ardor*, 101.

39 "home-made flute": Bishop, "Crusoe in England," *Poems*, 184.

41 "and I thought about that word *expense*": Graham, "Shroud," *Fast*, 11.

41 "is that which is lost": Frost, "Conversations on the Craft of Poetry," 856.

41 "it makes one's nose run": Bishop, "At the Fishhouses," *Poems*, 62.

42 "a cat at pranks": Smart, "Jubilate Agno," *Selected Poems*, 101.

42 "expanded explanation": Moore, "Feeling and Precision," *The Complete Prose*, 396.

43 "many chesty bureaucrats": DeLillo, *Underworld*, 794.

43 "that whistles up": Ibid., 14.

43 "how much summer": Ibid., 25.

43 "the voice is . . . mainly": Ibid., 43.

43 "Edgar turned . . . and saw himself": Ibid., 564.

44 "completely free of human presence": Ibid., 63.

45 "third ear": Nietzsche, *Beyond Good and Evil*, 152.

45 "there is *art*": Ibid., 153.

45 "I sensed knowledge in the football": DeLillo, *End Zone*, 37.

46 "commands the eye": DeLillo, *Underworld*, 820.

46   "it remains the author's": DeLillo, *End Zone*, 113.

46   "the words . . . commissioned": Ibid., 54.

46   "beauty fl[ying]": Ibid., 17.

47   "this smart soft caustic": Wallace, *Infinite Jest*, 114.

47   "He watched his own blood": Ibid., 979.

48   "My Life had stood": Dickinson, *Poems*, 722.

49   "Certain objects": Bollas, 17.

49   "seek, and ye shall find": Matthew 7:7.

49   "No contribution": Bollas, 81.

49   "people on whom": James, *Partial Portraits*, 390.

49   "We dream ourself": Bollas, 53.

49   "The distinction between the subject": Ibid., 31.

50   "Whoever *must* play": Carse, *Finite and Infinite Games*, 4.

50   "that weapon, self-protectiveness": Moore, "In This Age of Hard Trying, Nonchalance is Good and," *New Collected Poems*, 24.

50   "effectively takes a person": Carse, *Finite and Infinite Games*, 26.

51   "Self experiencing cannot be assumed": Bollas, 25.

51   "its own love back": Frost, "The Most of It," *Collected Poems, Prose & Plays*, 307.

51   "Love should be put into action": Bishop, "Chemin de Fer," *Poems*, 10.

52   "a new beginning": Nietzsche, *Thus Spoke Zarathustra*, 17.

52   "indrawn"; "everything was withdrawn"; "lengths and lengths"; "man-size"; "kite string?": Bishop, "The End of March," *Poems*, 199.

53   "My grandmother had kept": Robinson, 90.

53   "pull . . . in a pell-mell": Ibid., 91.

54   "medals with their ribbons"; "beard of wisdom": Bishop, "The Fish," *Poems*, 44.

54   "without any irritable reaching": Keats, 261.

54   "fill[s] up / the little rented boat": Bishop, "The Fish," *Poems*, 44.

54   "let[s] the fish go": Ibid., 44.

54   "a sort of artichoke"; "proto-dream-house"; "crypto-dream-house": Bishop, "The End of March," *Poems*, 199.

55   "*nothing,* / or nothing much"; "boring books"; "useless notes": Ibid., 200.

55   "one of the first things": Bishop, "Crusoe in England," *Poems*, 184.

55   "I'd have / nightmares": Ibid., 185.

56   "a House that seemed": Dickinson, *Poems*, 492.

56   "inhuman . . . veritable ocean": Stevens, "The Idea of Order at Key West," *Collected Poetry and Prose*, 105.

56 "put away [their] labor": Dickinson, *Poems*, 492.

57 "A word then": Whitman, "Song of Myself," *The Complete Poems*, 280.

57 "But no Man moved Me": Dickinson, *Poems*, 640.

58 "Man looking into the sea": Moore, "A Grave," *New Collected Poems*, 52.

58 "infinite speaker": Carse, *Finite and Infinite Games*, 110.

58 "we begin to see the narrative character": Ibid., 111.

58 "the wind was much too cold"; "The sun came out": Bishop, "The End of March," *Poems*, 200.

59 "something off behind the dunes": Ibid., 200.

III. TRANSGRESSION

64 "press back against": Stevens, "The Noble Rider and the Sound of Words," *Collected Poetry and Prose*, 665.

64 "Whose woods these are": Frost, "Stopping by the Woods on a Snowy Evening," *Collected Poems, Prose & Plays*, 207.

65 "the only voice": Naylor, 10.

66 "A young black girl stopped by the woods": Moss, "Interpretation of a Poem by Frost," *Rainbow Remnants*, 44.

66 "effuse my flesh": Whitman, "Song of Myself," *The Complete Poems*, 124.

67 "face eternally the brown": Moss, "Interpretation of a Poem by Frost," *Rainbow Remnants*, 44.

67 "the snow does not hypnotize": Ibid., 44.

68 "the promise that she bear Jim": Ibid., 44.

68 "What are we doing": Moss, "An Anointing," *Rainbow Remnants*, 11.

68 "dense": Moss, "Poem for my Mothers and Other Makers of Asafetida," Ibid., 28.

68 "vestiges . . . of evolution": Ibid., 29.

68 "no polyester, no rayon": Moss, "In the Pit of Crinoline Ruffles," *Tarzan Holler*, 6.

68 "long Caucasian history": Moss, "Second Grade Art: The Stunning Chances," Ibid., 47.

68 "a piece of Galileo's brain": Moss, "Beginning the Rock at Abbott School," Ibid., 7.

68 "common woman"; "common problem"; "her flesh"; "faithful, uncompromising": Moss, "Those Who Love Bones," Ibid., 11–12.

69 "swinging char"; "little lads, lynchers that were to be": McKay, "The Lynching," 177.

69   "No parent // of atrocity"; "baptizes by fire"; "becomes a holy ghost":
     Moss, "The Lynching," *Rainbow Remnants*, 45.

69   "the God . . . / does not glow"; "[its] thin moon-begot / shadow as
     mattress"; "something smoldering": Ibid., 46.

70   "the mind cheats": Moss, "Those Who Love Bones," *Tarzan Holler*, 12.

70   "to locate those zones": Wright, *Cooling Time*, 8.

70   "ardor comes before thought": Calasso, *Ardor*, 99.

71   "twinkle . . . from afar": Hesiod, *Theodicy*, *Works of Hesiod*, 73.

71   "the real literary experience": Lewis, 8.

71   "a sudden light": Shelley, *Frankenstein*, 31.

71   "I succeeded in discovering": Ibid., 32.

71   "I will not lead you on": Ibid.

72   "Our studies were never forced": Ibid., 21.

72   "Neither of us possessed": Ibid., 25.

72   "weakens your affections": Ibid., 34.

73   "ruined by reading": Schwartz, *Ruined by Reading*.

75   "the planet's most remorselessly": Wallace, *Infinite Jest*, 359.

75   "Of what a strange nature is knowledge!": Shelley, *Frankenstein*, 83.

76   "the strange system"; "division of property": Shelley, *Frankenstein*, 83.

76   "the power of truth": Douglass, *Narrative of the Life of Frederick Doug-
     lass*, *Autobiographies*, 42.

76   "Of my creation and creator": Shelley, *Frankenstein*, 83–84.

77   "By far the larger part": Douglass, *Narrative of the Life of Frederick
     Douglass*, *Autobiographies*, 15.

77   "As I read and contemplated": Ibid., 42–43.

78   "as much about uncertainty": Hayes, "Line 14: I Have the Same
     Name," *Space Between*, 64.

78   "the idea of liquidness": Ibid., 74.

79   "alone upon the lofty banks": Douglass, *Narrative of the Life of Freder-
     ick Douglass*, *Autobiographies*, 59.

79   "climb[s] . . . three staircases": Brontë, 116.

80   "All this I swallow": Whitman, "Song of Myself," *The Complete Poems*, 101.

81   "ha[s] only genius, wit, and taste"; "And what are you reading": Aus-
     ten, 36–37.

83   "What do I think of *Middlemarch*?": Dickinson, *Letters*, 506.

83   "knew many passages": Eliot, 8.

83   "many-volumed romances": Ibid., 3.

83   "weak opinions"; "political economy": Ibid., 9.

84 "'Seest thou'": Ibid., 16.
84 "When the two girls": Ibid., 20.
85 "really delightful marriage": Ibid., 10.
86 "those provinces of masculine knowledge": Ibid., 64.
86 "Dorothea is learning": Ibid., 65.
87 "He has got no red blood": Ibid., 70–71.
88 "shut her best soul in prison": Ibid., 426.
88 "look[ing] steadily at her husband's failure": Ibid., 365.
88 "abundant pen scratches": Ibid., 200.
88 "ante-rooms and winding passages": Ibid., 195.
89 "'Before I sleep'": Ibid., 477–78.
89 "hee for God only": Milton, *Paradise Lost*, *Complete Poems and Major Prose*, 285.
90 "she could not smite": Eliot, 481.
90 "What happens at the crucial moment": Calasso, *Ardor*, 62.
90 "intensity and greatness": Eliot, 8.

IV. INSIGHT

95 "a great many things [in English literature]": Stein, "What is English Literature," *Writings*, 200.
95 "get [it]self out of the way": Lewis, 19.
95 "I felt a palsy, here": Dickinson, *Letters*, 408.
95 "our culture . . . is what": Knausgaard, 11.
96 "globular" "men-wom[e]n": Hamilton, *Phaedrus*, *The Collected Dialogues of Plato*, 543.
96 "strength and energy": Ibid., 544.
96 "that fact is that [the soul longs]": Ibid., 545.
96 "something which there are": Shelley, *Phaedrus*, *The Symposium of Plato*, 59.
96 "something else which the soul": Jowett, *Phaedrus*, *The Dialogues of Plato*, 610.
96 "that for which it was searching": Stevens, "The Noble Rider and the Sound of Words," *Collected Poetry and Prose*, 661.
97 "stimulants, poultices, goads": Wright, *Deepstep*, 109.
97 "which organizes everything": Ashbery, "Self-Portrait in a Convex Mirror," *Self-Portrait*, 71.
97 "I went to the summit": Ammons, "For Harold Bloom," *The Complete Poems*, 645.

98　"Overall is beyond": Ammons, "Corsons Inlet," *The Complete Poems*, 92.

98　"narrow orders, limited tightness": Ibid., 95.

98　"the looser, wider forces": Ibid., 95.

98　"I went back down": Ammons, "For Harold Bloom," *The Complete Poems*, 645.

99　"it's a queer thing": Lawrence, 16.

99　"a dark forest"; "gods, strange gods"; "the courage to let them": Ibid., 22.

100　"point[s] to his books": Williams, *The Quick and the Dead*, 34.

100　"that other world": DeLillo, *End Zone*, 189.

100　"queerer than we suppose": Haldane, 298.

101　"I suspected there was a trick": Williams, "Escapes," *The Visiting Privilege*, 125.

101　"just a little different": Lerner, epigraph.

103　"grand, otherworldly": Bishop, "The Moose," *Poems*, 193.

103　"a gentle, auditory": Ibid., 191.

103　"There is no 'split'": Bishop, *Poems, Prose, and Letters*, 860.

104　"It must be Nova Scotia": Bishop, "Poem," *Poems*, 196.

105　"Heavens": Ibid.

105　"Our visions coincided": Ibid., 197.

106　"What good is a book": Nietzsche, *The Gay Science*, 148.

106　"an innavigable sea": Emerson, "Experience," *Essays & Poems*, 473.

106　"third rail,"; "unbroken draught": Bishop, "The Man-Moth," *Poems*, 17.

107　"must dazzle": Dickinson, *Poems*, 494.

107　"[peep] into the unseen": Wright, *Deepstep*, 8.

107　"in the direction": Ibid., 9.

107　"finite eyes": Dickinson, *Poems*, 361.

107　"has its centre": Moore, "Black Earth," *New Collected Poems*, 42.

107　"off behind"; "much too cold": Bishop, "The End of March," *Poems*, 200.

107　"many things [that] are unsettled"; "pending their settlement": Emerson, "Experience," *Essays & Poems*, 481.

107　"The first light of evening": Stevens, "Final Soliloquy of the Interior Paramour," *Collected Poetry and Prose*, 444.

107　"one late wicker-shaded"; "the waxing crescent-moon": Brock-Broido, "Pax Arcana," *Stay, Illusion*, 21.

107　"the light of an electric torch": Lewis, 8.

107 "a tongue of fire"; "a brimming / Saucer": Merrill, "The Broken Home," *Selected Poems*, 109.

107 "great goblets": Wright, *Deepstep*, 3.

107 "perfect! But—impossible": Bishop, "The End of March," *Poems*, 180.

107 "pours its abundance"; "in no way winces": Ammons, "The City Limits," *The Complete Poems*, 498.

107 "maya, illusion": Whitman, "Are You the New Person Drawn Toward Me?" *The Complete Poems*, 156.

107 "the translucent mistake": Moore, "The Jerboa," *New Collected Poems*, 103.

108 "letters are sounds we see," Howe, 139.

109 "invest [one's] life"; "the race [is] run": Merrill, "The Broken Home," *Selected Poems*, 109.

109 "screaming / 'Get up!'": Bishop, "Roosters," *Poems*, 36.

109 "you can't help that": Carroll, 90.

109 "Much Madness": Dickinson, *Poems*, 613.

109 "a broken drinking goblet"; "drink and be whole": Frost, "Directive," *Collected Poems, Prose & Plays*, 342.

109 "imaginary gardens": Moore, "Poetry," *New Collected Poems*, 27.

109 "counter-love, original response": Frost, "The Most of It," *Collected Poems, Prose & Plays*, 307.

109 "nothing happen": Auden, "In Memory of W. B. Yeats," *Selected Poems*, 82.

110 "in bitter manuscript remarks": Eliot, 273.

110 "ratified by collective agreement": Saussure, 15.

110 "the consequences which flow": Ibid., 68.

110 "a machine that moves": Wallace, "Forever Overhead," *Brief Interviews*, 13.

111 "There is, in fact": Stevens, "The Noble Rider and the Sound of Words," *Collected Poetry and Prose*, 662.

111 "that nobility which is"; "While I know": Ibid., 664.

112 "a release, if only"; "porous, resonant": Baker, 333.

112 "thoughts and feelings which, we are sure": Stevens, "The Noble Rider and the Sound of Words," *Collected Poetry and Prose*, 662.

112 "learn by going": Roethke, "The Waking," *The Collected Poems*, 104.

112 "The song and water"; "The sea . . . was merely": Stevens, "The Idea of Order at Key West," *Collected Poetry and Prose*, 105.

113 "Then we / As we beheld"; "the lights in the fishing boats"; "[master] the night": Ibid., 106.

114 "From this the poem springs": Stevens, "Notes Toward a Supreme Fiction," *Collected Poetry and Prose*, 332.

114 "where I end": Radiohead.

114 "Good as is discourse": Emerson, "Circles," *Essays & Poems*, 408.

114 "Surrendered sel[ves]"; "look and reflect"; "the air's glass / jail": Ammons, "Gravelly Run," *The Complete Poems*, 140.

115 "shift[s] a word or phrase": Preminger, 760.

115 "an octopus of ice": Moore, "An Octopus," *New Collected Poems*, 72.

115 "the biggest size of artificial pearls": Bishop, "Electrical Storm," *Poems*, 98.

115 "house[s] whose rooms": Smith, "Ash," *Wade in the Water*, 62.

115 "everything only connected": Bishop, "Over 2,000 Illustrations and a Complete Concordance," *Poems*, 58.

115 "the perpendiculars, / straight lines": Ammons, "Corsons Inlet," *The Complete Poems*, 92–93.

115 "most effective of the modes": Aristotle, 1327.

115 "everything got four sides": Naylor, 230.

116 "[The soul] is a wayfarer": Lawrence, 181.

116 "internal difference": Dickinson, *Poems*, 338.

117 "usefulness . . . has not been": Moss, "The Saint and the Modern Equivalent of the Miracle of Lactation," *Tarzan Holler*, 66.

117 "neat pseudonym": Merrill, "Morning Exercise," *A Scattering of Salts*, 18.

117 "the soul in her subtle sympathies": Lawrence, 182.

117 "Everything ripens": Hutchison, 8.

118 "Interactions are everything": Moss, Acknowledgments, *Tokyo Butter*, 131.

118 "resist[s] the intelligence": Stevens, "Man Carrying Thing," *Collected Poetry and Prose*, 306.

118 "tell[s] all the truth": Dickinson, *Poems*, 1089.

118 "MAKE SENSE": Merrill, *Scripts for the Pageant*, *The Changing Light at Sandover*, 337.

118 "through a loophole": Smith, *On Beauty*, 192.

120 "taint . . . / what is put out": Moss, "The Subculture of the Wrongfully Accused," *Tokyo Butter*, 39.

120 "something else": Ibid., 40.

120 "there is no use hesitating": Stein, *Four in America*, 131.

120 "Many lives changed": Moss, "The Subculture of the Wrongfully Accused," *Tokyo Butter*, 41.

121 "life and the memory": Bishop, "Poem," *Poems*, 197.

121 "Metaphor is a form": Moss, "The Subculture of the Wrongfully Accused," *Tokyo Butter*, 42.

122 "metaphor / is king": Ibid., 76.

123 "try[ing] each thing": Ashbery, "As One Put Drunk into the Packet-Boat," *Self-Portrait*, 1.

123 "words . . . of ourselves": Stevens, "The Idea of Order at Key West," *Collected Poetry and Prose*, 105.

V. CONCLUSIONS

128 "Once, self-determination": Moore, "Armor's Undermining Modesty," *New Collected Poems*, 188.

128 "From then on": Calasso, *Ardor*, 115.

128 "sounds leap[t] to": Howe, 139.

128 "occurrences, events": Ong, 31.

128 "exist[ing] only when": Ibid., 90.

128 "The sound of a word": Saussure, 116.

129 "the object in writing poetry": Frost, "The Figure a Poem Makes," *Collected Poems, Prose & Plays*, 776.

130 "below basic"; "simple and everyday": National Center for Education Statistics, "NAAL."

130 "use printed and written": National Assessment of Adult Literacy (NAAL), https://nces.ed.gov/naal/fr_definition.asp.

131 "According to a 2014 survey": "Highlights from the U.S. PIAAC Survey of Incarerated Adults: Their Skills, Work Experience, Education, and Training," https://nces.ed.gov/pubs2016/2016040.pdf, 6.

131 "make low-level"; "read short pieces": *Literacy Behind Prison Walls*, 17. https://nces.ed.gov/pubs94/94102.pdf.

132 "as it were estranged"; "Bailiffs, Debts"; "destined to hardships": Keats, 287.

132 "Call the world if you Please"; "there may be intelligences"; "they are not Souls"; "How then": Ibid., 288.

133 "a Place where the heart"; "as Various as the lives": Ibid., 289.

133 "in the most homely"; "I will call the *world*": Ibid., 288.

134 "What was it that nature would say": Emerson, "Nature," 15.

134 "To me the converging objects": Whitman, "Song of Myself," *The Complete Poems*, 82.

135 "The eager look": Dickinson, *Poems*, 338.

135 "The birds were like black letters": Clarke, 501.

135 "The pasture's crows": Wallace, *The Pale King*, 4.

136 "Where is a book": Barry, 44.

139 "The Child is the father": Wordsworth, "Intimations of Immortality," *Selected Poems and Prefaces*, 186.

139 "drop the Georgians": Lewis, 8.

Works Cited

Ammons, A. R. 2017. *The Complete Poems of A. R. Ammons*. New York: W. W. Norton.

Aristotle. 1941. *The Basic Works of Aristotle*. New York: Random House.

Ashbery, John. 1976. *Self-Portrait in a Convex Mirror*. New York: Penguin Books.

Auden, W. H. 1979. *Selected Poems*. New York: Vintage Books.

Austen, Jane. 2006. *Northanger Abbey*. New York: Penguin Books.

Baker, Robert. "What Do We Mean When We Talk About Transcendence? Plato and Virginia Woolf." *Philosophy and Literature* 43, no. 2 (October 2019): 312–33.

Barry, Lynda. 2009. *What It Is*. Montréal: Drawn & Quarterly.

Birkerts, Sven. 1994. *The Gutenberg Elegies: The Fate of Reading in an Electronic Age*. London: Faber & Faber.

Bishop, Elizabeth. 1994. *One Art*. New York: Farrar, Straus and Giroux.

Bishop, Elizabeth. 2011. *Poems*. New York: Farrar, Straus and Giroux.

Bishop, Elizabeth. 2008. *Poems, Prose, and Letters*. New York: Library of America.

Bollas, Christopher. 1992. *Being a Character: Psychoanalysis and Self Experience*. New York: Hill and Wang.

Brock-Broido, Lucie. 2013. *Stay, Illusion*. New York: Knopf.

Brontë, Charlotte. 1996. *Jane Eyre*. Boston and New York: Bedford/St. Martin's.

Brown, William Wells. 2004. *Clotel; or, The President's Daughter: A Narrative of Slave Life in the United States.* New York: Penguin.

Calasso, Roberto. 2002. *Literature and the Gods.* Translated by Tim Parks. New York: Knopf.

Calasso, Roberto. 2014. *Ardor.* Translated by Richard Dixon. New York: Farrar, Straus and Giroux.

Carroll, L. 1909. *Alice's Adventures in Wonderland.* New York: Macmillan.

Carse, James P. 1986. *Finite and Infinite Games: A Vision of Life as Play and Possibility.* New York: Free Press.

Carse, James P. 2009. *The Religious Case Against Belief.* New York: Penguin.

Cervantes Saavedra, Miguel de. 2003. *Don Quixote.* Translated by Edith Grossman. New York: Ecco.

Chabon, Michael. 2012. *Telegraph Avenue.* New York: HarperCollins.

Chai, Eleanor. 2016. *Standing Water.* New York: Farrar, Straus and Giroux.

Costikyan, Greg. 2002. "I Have No Words & I Must Design: Toward a Critical Vocabulary for Games." Computer Games and Digital Cultures Conference Proceedings. http://www.costik.com/nowords2002.pdf

DeLillo, Don. 1986. *End Zone.* New York: Penguin.

DeLillo, Don. 2007. *Underworld.* New York: Scribner.

Dickinson, Emily. 1986. *The Letters of Emily Dickinson.* Cambridge, Mass.: Belknap Press of Harvard University Press.

Dickinson, Emily. 1998. *The Poems of Emily Dickinson.* Cambridge, Mass.: Belknap Press of Harvard University Press.

Donne, John. 1974. *The Complete English Poems of John Donne.* New York: St. Martin's Press.

Douglass, Frederick. 1994. *Autobiographies.* New York: Library of America.

Eliot, George. 1994. *Middlemarch.* New York: Penguin.

Emerson, Ralph W. 1996. *Essays & Poems.* New York: Library of America.

Frost, Robert. 1995. *Collected Poems, Prose & Plays.* New York: Library of America.

Goodell, William. 1853. *The American Slave Code in Theory and Practice.* New York: American and Foreign Anti-Slavery Society.

Graham, Jorie. 2018. *Fast.* New York: HarperCollins.

Haldane, J. B. S. 1928. *Possible Worlds, and Other Papers.* New York and London: Harper & Brothers.

Hamilton, Edith. 1985. *The Collected Dialogues of Plato: Including the Letters.* New York: Princeton University Press.

Hayes, Terrance. 2018. *To Float in the Space Between.* Seattle and New York: Wave Books.

Hesiod. 2005. *Works of Hesiod and the Homeric Hymns*. Translated by Daryl Hine. Chicago: University of Chicago Press.

Hirshfield, Jane. 2015. *Ten Windows: How Great Poems Transform the World*. New York: Knopf.

Howe, Susan. 1993. *The Birth-Mark: Unsettling the Wilderness in American Literary History*. Hanover, Germany: Wesleyan University Press.

Hurston, Zora Neale. 2000. *Their Eyes Were Watching God*. New York: HarperCollins.

Hutchinson, Ishion. 2016. *House of Lords and Commons*. New York: Farrar, Straus and Giroux.

James, Henry. 1888. *Partial Portraits*. New York: Macmillan.

James, Henry. 1974. *Letters*. Cambridge, Mass.: Belknap Press of Harvard University Press.

James, William. 1992. *Writings, 1878–1899*. New York: Library of America.

Jowett, Benjamin. 1892. *The Dialogues of Plato: Charmides. Lysis. Laches. Protagoras. Euthydemus. Cratylus. Phaedrus. Ion. Symposium*. Oxford and London: Oxford University Press.

Kafka, Franz. 2016. *Letters to Friends, Family, and Editors*. Translated by Richard Winston and Clara Winston. New York: Schocken Books.

Keats, John. 1959. *Selected Poems and Letters*. Boston: Houghton Mifflin.

Knausgaard, Karl Ove. 2018. *My Struggle*. Translated by D. Bartlett and M. Aitken. Vol. 6. New York: Farrar, Straus and Giroux.

Lawrence, D. H. 1977. *Studies in Classic American Literature*. New York: Penguin Books.

Lerner, Ben. 2014. *10:04*. New York: Farrar, Straus and Giroux.

Lewis, C. S. 2012. *An Experiment in Criticism*. Cambridge, U.K.: Cambridge University Press.

Manguel, Alberto. 1997. *A History of Reading*. New York: Penguin.

McHenry, Elizabeth. 2002. *Forgotten Readers: Recovering the Lost History of African American Literary Societies*. Durham, N.C.: Duke University Press.

McKay, Claude. 2004. *Complete Poems*. Urbana: University of Illinois Press.

Merrill, James. 1992a. *The Changing Light at Sandover*. New York: Knopf.

Merrill, James. 1992b. *Selected Poems, 1946–1985*. New York: Knopf.

Merrill, James. 1995. *A Scattering of Salts*. New York: Knopf.

Milton, John. 2003. *Complete Poems and Major Prose*. Indianapolis: Hackett.

Moore, Marianne. 1986. *The Complete Prose of Marianne Moore*. New York: Viking.

Moore, Marianne. 2017. *New Collected Poems of Marianne Moore*. New York: Farrar, Straus and Giroux.

Moss, Thylias. 1991. *Rainbow Remnants in Rock Bottom Ghetto Sky*. New York: Persea Books.

Moss, Thylias. 1998. *Last Chance for the Tarzan Holler*. New York: Persea Books.

Moss, Thylias. 2006. *Tokyo Butter: A Search for Forms of Deirdre*. New York: Persea Books.

Nabokov, Vladimir. 2016. *Lectures on Don Quixote*. Boston: Houghton Mifflin Harcourt.

National Center for Education Statistics. "National Assessment of Adult Literacy (NAAL)." U.S. Department of Education. https://nces.ed.gov /naal/kf_demographics.asp.

Naylor, Gloria. 1989. *Mama Day*. New York: Vintage Books.

Nietzsche, Friedrich Wilhelm. 2000. *Human, All Too Human, I*. Translated by Gary Handwerk. Palo Alto, Calif.: Stanford University Press.

Nietzsche, Friedrich Wilhelm. 2001. *The Gay Science*. Translated by Josefine Nauckhoff. Cambridge and New York: Cambridge University Press.

Nietzsche, Friedrich Wilhelm. 2006. *Thus Spoke Zarathustra*. Translated by Adrian Del Caro. Cambridge and New York: Cambridge University Press.

Nietzsche, Friedrich Wilhelm. 2013. *Human, All Too Human, II*. Translated by Gary Handwerk. Palo Alto, Calif.: Stanford University Press.

Nietzsche, Friedrich Wilhelm. 2014. *Beyond Good and Evil/On the Genealogy of Morality*. Translated by Adrian Del Caro. Palo Alto, Calif.: Stanford University Press.

O'Hara, Frank. 1964. *Lunch Poems*. San Francisco: City Lights Books.

Ong, Walter J. 2013. *Orality and Literacy: 30th Anniversary Edition*. London and New York: Routledge.

Phillips, Adam. 1994. *On Kissing, Tickling, and Being Bored: Psychoanalytic Essays on the Unexamined Life*. Cambridge, Mass.: Harvard University Press.

Preminger, Alex, and T. V. F. Brogan. 1993. *The New Princeton Encyclopedia of Poetry and Poetics*. Princeton, N.J.: Princeton University Press.

Radiohead. 2003. "Where I End and You Begin." In *Hail to the Thief*. Nashville: Warner Chappell Music Publishing Ltd.

Robinson, Marilynne. 2004. *Housekeeping*. New York: Farrar, Straus and Giroux.

Roethke, Theodore. 1991. *The Collected Poems of Theodore Roethke*. New York: Anchor Books.

Rose, Gillian. 2011. *Love's Work*. New York: New York Review Books.

Saunders, George. 2013. *Tenth of December: Stories*. New York: Random House.

Saussure, Ferdinand de. 1983. *Course in General Linguistics*. Translated by Roy Harris. Chicago: Open Court.

Schwartz, Lynne Sharon. 1996. *Ruined by Reading: A Life in Books*. Boston: Beacon Press.

Shelley, Mary Wollstonecraft. 1996. *Frankenstein*. New York: W. W. Norton.

Shelley, Percy Bysshe. 2002. *The Symposium of Plato*. New York: St. Augustine's Press.

Smart, Christopher. 1990. *Selected Poems*. London and New York: Penguin.

Smith, Tracy K. 2018. *Wade in the Water*. Minneapolis: Graywolf Press.

Smith, Zadie. 2005. *On Beauty*. New York: Penguin.

Spiotta, Dana. 2016. *Innocents and Others*. New York: Scribner.

Stein, Gertrude. 1947. *Four in America*. New Haven and New York: Yale University Press.

Stein, Gertrude. 1998. *Writings, 1932–1946*. New York: Library of America.

Stevens, Wallace. 1997. *Collected Poetry and Prose*. New York: Library of America.

Thoreau, Henry David. 2004. *Walden*. Princeton, N.J.: Princeton University Press.

Walker, David. 1830. *Walker's Appeal, in Four Articles; Together with a Preamble, to the Coloured Citizens of the World, but in Particular, and Very Expressly, to Those of the United States of America, Written in Boston, State of Massachusetts, September 28, 1829*. https://docsouth.unc.edu/nc/walker/walker.html.

Wallace, David Foster. 1996. *Infinite Jest*. Boston: Little, Brown.

Wallace, David Foster. 1999. *Brief Interviews with Hideous Men*. Boston: Little, Brown.

Wallace, David Foster. 2010. *Everything and More: A Compact History of Infinity*. New York: W. W. Norton.

Wallace, David Foster. 2011. *The Pale King*. Boston, Little: Brown.

Whitman, Walt. 1975. *The Complete Poems*. Harmondsworth, U.K.: Penguin.

Williams, Joy. 2010. *The Quick and the Dead*. New York: Knopf.

Williams, Joy. 2016. *The Visiting Privilege: New and Collected Stories*. New York: Knopf.

Winnicott, D. W. 2005. *Playing and Reality*. London and New York: Routledge.

Wordsworth, William. 1965. *Selected Poems and Prefaces*. Boston: Houghton Mifflin.

Wright, C. D. 1998. *Deepstep Come Shining*. Port Townsend, Wash.: Copper Canyon Press.

Wright, C. D. 2005. *Cooling Time: An American Poetry Vigil*. Port Townsend, Wash.: Copper Canyon Press.

Acknowledgments

I am grateful to many people for helping this book come to be. Jonathan Galassi, dream-weaver, accepted it. Robert Baker, Luke Carson, Ellen Levy, Heather Roberts, and Lee Shea were its generous first readers. Michelle Dowd, Cassander Smith, and Steve Tedeschi offered specialist consultations, though they are not responsible for what I did with them.

My family, most especially my husband, Randy, gave me courage to write the book. The young readers in our lives, Ingrid, Jack, Xander, Zeke, and Conrad, reminded me of where it all began.

This book is dedicated with gratitude to Robert Baker. In our many conversations about it, his "speech had the form of listening."